A TASTE OF CHINA

A Taste of CHINA

JAMES BALLINGALL

Franklin Watts

NEW YORK

1984

Printed in Great Britain

First published in the United Kingdom in 1984
by John Murray (Publishers) Ltd

First United States publication 1984
by Franklin Watts Inc.,
387 Park Avenue South
New York, NY 10016

ISBN: 0–531–09768–4
Library of Congress Catalog card number: 84–50570

Contents

Illustrations

Drawings by Anne Ballingall

Photographs reproduced by permission of:-
* Joe Whitlock Blundell
† Hsinhua News Agency
‡ Anglo-Chinese Educational Institute

The Chinese Dynasties

Xia	c.2100–1600 BC
Shang	c.1600–1100 BC
Zhou	c.1100–221 BC
Western Zhou c.1100–770 BC	
Eastern Zhou c.770–221 BC	
Qin	221–206 BC
Han	206 BC–AD 220
Western Han 206 BC– AD 24	
Eastern Han 24–220	
Three Kingdoms	220–280
Jin	265–420
Southern and Northern	420–589
Sui	581–618
Tang	618–979
Song	960–1279
Northern Song 960–1127	
Southern Song 1127–1279	
Yuan	1271–1368
Ming	1368–1644
Quing	1644–1911
The Republic of China	1911–49
The People's Republic of China	1949–

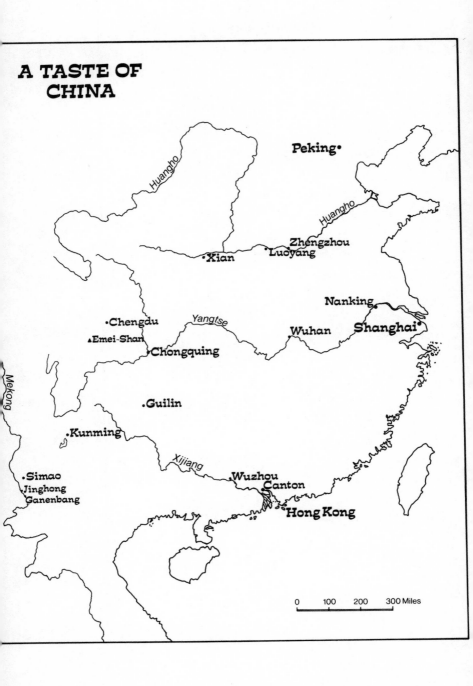

A TASTE OF CHINA

Peking•

Huangho

Huangho

Zhengzhou
•Xian •Luoyang

Nanking•
•Chengdu   Yangtse   Wuhan   Shanghai•
▲Emei-Shan
            Chongquing

•Guilin

•Kunming

Mekong

Xijiang

•Simao   Wuzhou•
Jinghong   Canton•
Ganenbang
                Hong Kong

0   100   200   300 Miles

*Dedicated
with gratitude to
my family*

PART ONE

1

Fragrant Harbour: Hong Kong

THEY SAY that landing in Hong Kong is one of the great air experiences of the world. Not, however, if you have a seat in the middle of the plane. Some cities grow on you. Hong Kong hits you between the eyes. From the moment you smack down on the runway stretching like a concrete finger out into the sea, and taxi towards the soaring skyscrapers, you're left in no doubt that you've arrived.

Hong Kong – 'fragrant harbour' – is a city of extremes. The strong flourish while the poor struggle to survive. It is a concrete jungle where the law of capitalism reigns supreme. Four and a half million people cram on to a small island called Victoria, after the queen, and the mainland peninsula called Kowloon, or nine dragons, after the hills which form it. In just over a century an unknown, barren chunk of rock off the mainland of China, surrounded by deep water, bombarded by fierce tropical typhoons springing out of the South China Sea, has become the flourishing economic showpiece of the capitalist world, and this on the doorstep and with the unspoken approval of Communist China.

It is a magical place in the shadow of the Orient, where anything is possible. Traditional bat-winged junks float among the ferries which ply across the deep water sound separating the island from the mainland. Destroyers compete with cargo boats for space at the docks, while the huge ocean-going tankers rest in deep water among the outlying islands. A mass of humanity fills the streets. Huge neon signs crowd the air, raw and ugly in the plain light of day.

Ask directions and the people will be too busy to help you, buy a hamburger and you will pay the price of a full meal, look for a room and you'll end up in a tiny dormitory on the sixteenth floor of a dirty apartment block. Space and time here are at a premium. Many tourists initially recoil at this seething ants' nest. Some of course have enough money not to notice. The Peninsula Hotel has a fleet of Rolls Royces ready to meet its guests at the airport. In Hong Kong it is not enough merely to make money, you must spend it, and as ostentatiously as possible. Flashing by in their brand-new sports cars the whizz kids broadcast a message: 'Live fast, live dangerously.' For those that can stand it, the rewards are there. Fortunes are won and lost daily.

There is a darker side to the city; a shadow behind the neon signs which your eyes, dazzled by the glamour of arrival, don't at first perceive. Although massive projects have given homes to half the city's bursting population, there is a difference in the way people live here. They live on top of each other, rather than next to each other. In addition, thousands of illegal immigrants, not officially recognised by the authorities, have nowhere to go. Soldiers and police patrolling the coast and border have reduced the illicit stream from mainland China to a trickle. The island would be swamped and sink below the waves like an over-loaded ark if they did not. In a single month, May 1962, when the Chinese Government temporarily opened its borders to the colony, 50,000 immigrants poured across. They come still, floating across the shark-ridden sea on inflated pigs' bladders, risking their lives in the hope of better things on the far side.

Police have also tried to clamp down on the opium trade. Drug addiction, especially among the young, is frighteningly prevalent, but it is hard to stamp out a trade upon whose back the whole community was established. In many ways, Hong Kong has reason to be ashamed of its past. In some ways it has reason to be ashamed of its present. Whatever it is, it is a product of humanity: man-made in nearly every respect. The whole community bears the stamp 'Made in Hong Kong'. Man has the power to change his environment. Six-laned concrete tentacles spread out over the island and under the sound. Soaring scrapers rise up into the sky, but occasionally, still, nature asserts itself and devil winds come roaring out of the south to send one of these great structures sliding down the hill. I find a hotel dormitory on the sixteenth floor of one of these buildings. Inside all the occupants are crammed around a little television. So much for the cheerful bonhomie of my fellow travellers. I am somewhat appeased, however, to find that they are watching Mario Puzo's *The Godfather* – a film the Chinese would understand only too well.

When the film is over, I get into conversation with a bearded German who has just come out of China.

'They're great people,' he says. 'The greatest people on earth, and it's not impossible to get there. You can get an entry permit from China Travel Service. Hop on a train and you're there. You're on your own. You and a billion Chinese. It's a once in a lifetime opportunity, and it could be stopped at any time. Individualism isn't exactly their cup of tea, and who needs people like us wandering around their country? We contribute as little as we can to the economy, get to places we shouldn't go to, say things we shouldn't say to people we shouldn't be talking to. Oh yes, there's a government directive forbidding contact with foreigners, but you'll never learn Chinese anyway, so it needn't worry you.'

I spend the next day applying for my entry permit and looking around the shops. Hong Kong is the only place in the world where you can get an individual (as opposed to a group) entry permit to visit the People's Republic of China, and even here it's not guaranteed. Christmas is in the crisp air. People wrap presents in pretty paper and coloured ribbons. Carols ring out above the noise of the bargaining. A newspaper tells me that England is in the grip of the worst winter this century. I won't be able to celebrate Christmas this year (1981). I won't be in a Christian country.

In the evening I transfer to a hilltop Youth Hostel. Beneath me the town is a blaze of light, each ship at anchor a dot of colour on the water. A red beacon on the peak behind flashes a warning to the planes that fill the night sky. The eye passes beyond this glittering enclave to the silent bulk of the Chinese mainland beyond, where sleeps the dragon.

The next day I meet an old schoolfriend at the Connaught building. This stands in the heart of Victoria, dominating the waterfront. A central symbol of the Hong Kong community, its distinctive round-windowed design has earned it a number of nicknames. Those that regard it with affection call it 'the Swiss cheese', and those with less affection 'the building of a thousand orifices', or words to that effect.

We go to an excellent restaurant in the bowels of the earth, before collecting the car from the rooftop car park. In Hong Kong you have to get used to living on unnatural levels. You work on the fortieth floor of an office block, have lunch in a basement restaurant, walk back along a raised pedestrian way, and travel home on a double decker bus through the underground tunnel to your high-rise apartment block. Only if you are very lucky will your feet ever touch the ground. Even the horses at the Jockey Club are exercised on the roofs.

We drive up Mount Victoria, past the cricket club carved into its crest, and hurtle down the hairpins on the far side into Repulse Bay. While we are having afternoon tea on the white-arched verandah of the Repulse Bay Hotel (one of the last survivals of the old colonial days), my friend points to a lonely yacht out in the bay.

'Do you see that yacht? It belongs to the richest man on the island. The Taipan. It's so big it can't dock with the other boats at the jetty, but anchors out in the deep water of the bay.'

Despite their commercial success, many Hong Kong Chinese are still influenced by their old ways and superstitions. The head of the great trading houses are still known as Taipans or supreme leaders, the violent tropical storms are still known as devil winds or typhoons, and the lives of the people are still governed by joss, or luck. Before settling into a new home the first guest any Chinese family will invite round is the Feng Shui man. He will make sure that you do not live on the head of a dragon, that your furniture is correctly aligned with the paths of the spirits, that your rooms will not trap evil forces, or your mirrors frighten away benevolent ones. He will assure your future happiness in your new home. On an island where the devil winds regularly used to level all the local villages, the spiritual surveyor is an important man. It is not just the old

wives who use him. Few Chinese businessmen will take any
important commercial step without first asking their Feng Shui
what the future holds for them. This could explain Hong Kong's
uncanny success in the business world.

We have a final cream cake and move on to the colourful
clothes market at Stanley, where I buy a padded skiing jacket to
keep me warm in China, and part from my friend.

I wake at seven the next day, eager to get under way, and kick
John, an American I have made friends with at the Youth
Hostel, out of bed. We both want to go to China, get along very
well, and have decided to set off together. He is a bearded
thirty-five-year-old accountant from Pennsylvania, and the son
of a vicar. After thirty-five years of listening to sermons and
looking at accounts he has decided there is more to life than
numbers and religion. There is also England. He has left his job,
left home, and bought himself a student card. 'I am now a
Student of Life,' he explains. In his new-found capacity he has
discovered that certain other countries lie between California
and England and set out to visit them all. China is the first one
he has come across, and I, perhaps, the first Englishman. I am
thus, in his eyes, the ideal travelling companion. As he put it
yesterday, 'I figure China's the sort of place a guy could use
some company, and I figure China's the sort of place a guy
would have trouble finding some company, so why don't you
and me join forces for a while.'

'Seems a fine idea to me,' I replied, and so it did, yesterday,
but this morning, anxious to get under way, it takes me five
minutes to pack, while it takes John an hour and a half. This
bodes ill. I am a minimal packer while he is obviously a maxi-
mal one. I take pleasure in carrying as little as possible and
making one article serve a number of purposes. He takes
pleasure in having something for every eventuality. He's a great
gadget man. As I chivvy him along he keeps muttering, 'A place
for everything and everything in its place. I'm a very ordered
person.'

'Well in that case you won't mind me telling you what to do,'
I say. 'Hurry up.'

At last he zips his rucksack up, and ties a large 'real' sponge to
a strap at the back. As he sways down the hill in front of me,
sponge swinging from side to side like a tail, he looks for all the

world like a giant tortoise carrying his home on his back – and I suppose he is. He's slow enough for one.

We wait another two hours for his visa to come through, before reaching the station. The two local trains to the border have gone, so we are forced to catch the express which goes straight through to Canton in three hours. It is six times as expensive and three times as fast as the local train, thus affording John an excellent opportunity to exercise his powers of accountancy.

2

The Gateway and the Key: Canton

SO WE ARE on our way to Ancient China, not jogging across the border on the back of an old mule, not battling between unscalable Himalayan peaks with weary Sherpas, not poling upriver on a shaky sampan, nor sailing into port on the deck of a Chinese junk, but sitting back in the luxury of an express train. It's more like being in an aeroplane than a train. The passengers sit in individual seats facing in the same direction, all pointing at a television screen. On reaching Canton, the officials swivel the seats round through 180° and head back.

Despite our anachronistic arrival I feel a growing sense of excitement as we pull up beside the railway platform in Canton. Canton, or Guangzhou, as the Chinese now call it, has a long and chequered history. Its strategic position at the end of an estuary off the South China Sea, on a flat strip of coastline below the inland hills, made it a natural focus for trade and settlement in the south. Today it is the capital of Guangdong province and has a population of two million. In Imperial times it formed one of the two great gateways to China. While traders with strings of camels pursued their long and lonely journey through the deserts of the north to Xian, the landgate, the seagoing merchants would bring their wares to Canton, the watergate, in the south. Canton rose to fame over a thousand years ago under the Tang Emperors, though its origins stretch back a further

9

thousand years. It has flourished over the centuries when Hong Kong was no more than a barren rock obstructing the mouth of its estuary.

The Chinese have always restricted the access of foreigners to their country. Canton was given a trading monopoly on the South China coast and has always been China's most important link with the outside world. Millions of Chinese people scattered round the globe issued from Canton and regard it as home, and that is why nearly all the Chinese restaurants in the West serve Cantonese food. Today, as transport by air becomes an increasingly popular alternative to transport by sea, and as China opens up further markets to the West, Canton is losing its pre-eminent position. It is, however, the town in which modern China has chosen to hold its biannual world trade fair, and for most visitors, remains the gateway to the nation.

The history of Canton is intimately connected to that of Hong Kong. Events which took place on its waterfront in the last century led directly to the founding of the British Colony. The story is not a pretty one and shows British Imperialism at its worst. China has never had close trading links with the rest of the world. Traditionally the Chinese have viewed merchants with scorn. In the past, however, their virtual monopoly of two products enabled them to rock the economy of the world. Over two thousand years ago they sent out silk overland from Xian along a path which became synonymous with its product: 'the silk road'. China gave the world silk and took in exchange gold, amassing reserves, it is said, of five million ounces. So serious did the drain become that the Emperor Tiberius, in the other great capital of the ancient world, Rome, had to ban the wearing of silk at the time of Christ. In the last century China supplied the world with tea, and accepted only silver in return. The English, being the greatest traders (and perhaps tea drinkers) of the nineteenth century suffered particularly from this imbalance and cast around for another commodity in which to trade. China, however, proved horribly self-sufficient. All we could find to tempt the Oriental palate was the illicit pleasure of opium. Having made this opening, our traders did everything they could to exploit it. They created a captive market, and made fortunes at their prisoners' expense. The

East India Company turned the plains of Bengal red with
poppies. Jardine Matheson and the other Hong Kong trading
houses built financial empires on the backs of opium addicts.
Britain, who banned the sale of the drug at home, condoned it
round the other side of the world.

Peking sent down an official called Commissioner Lin, to
curb the corruption in the south and stamp out the illegal trade.
He wrote a delightful letter to Queen Victoria in which, while
he correctly gauged the importance of his tea, he sadly mis-
judged the status of our nation. China tended to regard foreign
traders as emissaries bringing tribute from vassal states:

> The kings of your country by a tradition handed down from
> generation to generation have always been noted for their polite-
> ness and submissiveness ... we are delighted with the way in
> which the honourable rulers of your country deeply understand
> the grand principles and are grateful for the celestial grace ... Of
> all that China exports to foreign countries there is not a single thing
> which is not beneficial to the people ... Take tea and rhubarb, for
> example, the foreign countries could not get along for a single day
> without them. If China cuts off these benefits with no sympathy for
> those who are to suffer, then what can the barbarians rely upon to
> keep themselves alive?

Lin then went on to contrast the benefits of tea with the evils
of opium and exhorted Her Majesty to stop the trade. Indeed he
went further. He confiscated the traders' opium stocks, dis-
solved them, and poured them into the sea, having first begged
pardon from the spirit of the ocean. Far from securing an opium
truce, however, all he succeeded in doing was to start an opium
war. Britain, the little vassal state, rudely sent out gun-boats to
support its traders, which, to the shame of the Chinese, proved
invincible. In 1842, they were forced to sign the first of the
'unequal treaties', ceding Hong Kong to Britain and giving her
rights in Canton, Shanghai and three other 'treaty ports' as well
as compensation for lost 'cargo'. Thus did the foreign nations
begin to apportion up China. Within twenty years Britain had
marched on the capital, Peking. In 1898 Britain 'leased', rent-
free for a hundred years, an area of mainland opposite Victoria
Island, which we called the 'New Territories'. Today, China
seeks to reclaim her territory. As the end of the lease

approaches, the fate of Hong Kong is very much in the balance.

Back in Canton, where it all began, I step off the train with all the childish enthusiasm of an eight-year-old on his first trip abroad. There's a freshness and newness that dispels world-weary cynicism and restores a sense of wonder. The faces of the people, freed from the tyranny of the mirror and the pretence of make-up, glow with health, and their eyes sparkle with friendly interest. The air is crisp and cool like an English Christmas. It flows into your lungs, restoring life to limbs grown tired from the heat of the tropics. Tchaikovsky booms out over old-fashioned station loudspeakers tied with string to the pillars. We make our way to the customs officials standing quietly to attention by their desks, in plain green uniforms unrelieved except for a red star on the peaked cap. I sign a form saying I do not possess any firearms, or inflammable or politic-ally sensitive material (including Bibles.) They are much too polite to doubt my word by actually checking my rucksack, and motion me through.

John and I change some money and pass through the gates of the station to find ourselves standing on the steps of an enor-mous square. Huge grey buildings surround it – a legacy from China's period of Soviet influence in the fifties. A cold wind whistles through the void, sweeping down from the chill moun-tains of Tibet or perhaps the frozen steppes of Asia. The square is a vast expanse of concrete. Where the English would have a garden, the French a fountain and the Germans a statue, the Chinese have nothing. This is a square built for the sake of being a square. But that does not mean that it is empty. It is full – full, not of buses or of cars, but of people, hurrying from one end of the vast expanse to the other. It is a sea of blue, for they are all wearing the famous Mao suit: square-cut blue jacket buttoning up the middle, with two large front pockets, and baggy trousers. It is loose-fitting to allow for more clothes underneath. I wanted to laugh when I first saw the bank clerk wearing two sweaters, a padded jacket and a track-suit top under his Mao suit. Now I realise the wisdom of his ways.

Immediately two facts about China impress themselves upon me: size and population. This, the third biggest country in the world after the Soviet Union and Canada, supports a quarter of the world's population.

'Come on,' I say to John, 'let's find the hotel, I'm getting cold.'

We venture into the mass and are immediately swallowed up. The people are not as small or slant-eyed as I expected them to be, but there are still many reasons to set us apart. You feel here isn't another fair-haired, round-eyed foreigner within a thousand miles of you, and you're probably right.

Finding anything in China is a tremendous problem. It is impossible to find or read signs, or even get directions from locals. There are too many barriers to be crossed. In other countries your halting attempts to speak the local language are met with encouragement. Here they are met with incredulity. Most Chinese can understand that some strange people are unable to speak their language, but few seem to understand our efforts to learn it. They assume they are talking to a lunatic and, as often as not, will turn tail and run. A fair-haired giant grunting and waving his arms about in a threatening manner is not to be trifled with. If, despite all this, you still manage to get to your destination, you are likely to walk straight past it, for it won't have a name written up. Your only hope is to get explicit directions and sketch maps from other travellers who have been that way. Rather like the early sailing ships on long ocean-going voyages, travellers whose paths cross in China always stop to exchange news. There are few enough such ships, so you are always pleased to see them. In China you look out for your fellow traveller; elsewhere you avoid him.

The hotel should not be too difficult to find. In any town you are allowed to visit there will only be one or perhaps two hotels in which you are allowed to stay. You will never get into a local hotel. The owner knows that you aren't allowed to stay there, and that he will probably lose his licence if you do. Try as you may, all you will receive is a politely negative smile. Provoked by this inscrutable smiling exterior, travellers are sometimes goaded into argument, if not to get in, at least to get some sort of emotional response from the grinning mask in front of them. But to raise your voice here is only to demean yourself. The Chinese in China are a marvellously polite people – and what are manners but a way of disguising, or at least formalising, emotions? It is a true saying that you need never be polite to a friend, so don't be misled by Chinese courtesy. Certainly they want to be nice to you and to give the best impression of their country, but they also want to keep you at a distance – or, at least the authorities do. There is a government directive forbidding the people to associate with foreign guests, and the government in China is everywhere.

Secrecy is a part of the Chinese way of life. From the days when they built a great wall to defend their country, and even before, they have sought to shelter from the world's gaze, previously because they felt they were ahead of the rest of us, now perhaps because they fear they have been left behind. The gates of China have been closed for two thousand years, but now, while I stand on the doorstep wondering how I can get into this forbidden country, they open a chink and a voice calls: 'Come in, come in and see for yourself.' For the first time China has invited guests into its homeland. At such a sensitive moment we must not rush in precipitously, or the gates will swing shut behind us. The Chinese very definitely want to learn from the West, but they've waited two thousand years and they're in no hurry now.

It would be a mistake to think that the Chinese are so very different from us, or that they lack emotions. They feel things in the same way as we do and within their own households seem very affectionate. Even with us they are bursting with curiosity, only they are too inhibited to show it. When you walk down the street you think the people are ignoring you, but turn round quickly and you'll find that everyone behind is looking at you. You don't get those dreadful 'hellos' echoing after you as happens elsewhere in South East Asia or people pawing at your arm for attention in the shops, but just stop for a minute to get your shoe repaired by a wayside cobbler, and you will be surrounded by a crowd of people. Communication is impossible. You have to do your best with paper messages carefully written out in advance to cover your basic contingencies. You can't always get close enough even for this. Sometimes they won't look at the message or make any attempt to understand the simplest of gestures. They assume or pretend they can't help; they smile, wave their hand in front of their mouth, and close their mind to you. No amount of gesticulating will convince them that they can help you if they will only make the mental leap. You are from another world, you are beyond comprehension. Perhaps this is just their way of obeying the government directive not to associate with foreigners. One never knows but one normally finds someone to help in the end.

John starts off very optimistically: 'Don't worry, there's one language everyone understands,' he says. 'Money. Money talks.'

But he's wrong. We stride off confidently to the large building opposite the station and slide across our message saying 'We want to stay here tonight'. The receptionist shakes his head and points to the door. 'Just watch this,' murmurs John, getting out a wad of notes and waving them under the Chinaman's nose. He in turn gets out a sheet of stamps. We are in the local post office.

Money does not talk very loudly over here, or at least, not as loudly as the government. If a Chinaman won't let you stay at his hotel or post office it's not a matter of price, it's a matter of rules and regulations. He refuses, not because he doesn't want you to stay, but because it is forbidden. To attempt to argue your way in is unfair to him. To offer him money is insulting. It is not a question of money.

Even when you find the official hotel your troubles are not over. It may take an hour's negotiating before you get a bed. Here, two government directives apply. Foreign guests must have first-class treatment. Foreign guests must pay Western prices. Both ideas take a little getting used to. For the budget traveller seeing South East Asia on a shoe-string, deluxe hotel bedrooms and soft train sleepers are an unexpected and un-wanted extravagance. To find London prices in the middle of Asia comes as a rude surprise. The government would argue that you are used to paying such prices for such things in the West and thus it should come as no surprise to pay similar prices here. Why should you benefit from one of the lowest costs of living in the world? Package-deal holidaymakers on group tours with China Travel Service accept this without thinking, for it is what they are used to; the Chinese, however, in granting individual visas to budget travellers, will have to get used to a new type of foreign friend. Their assumption that all West-erners are necessarily wealthy is no longer true. There are various good reasons why different people should pay different prices for the same thing. One principle states: 'From each according to his means, to each according to his needs,' but when you find yourself paying twenty times as much for something as the person in front of you, it's very difficult not to feel there's a little unfair discrimination going on.

Your first problem on arriving at a hotel is convincing the management that you don't want a bedroom with bathroom attached. To this end, the first message I normally push across the counter is: 'I do not want a bedroom with a bathroom attached. I want a bed in a dormitory, please.'

Naturally they will tell you that they don't have a dormitory. This is where prior information gained from fellow travellers can be useful. In a difficult situation, Chinese officials regard lying as a perfectly acceptable negotiating technique. I ignore their reply, and carry on with my dormitory attack. Once the existence of the dormitory has finally been admitted they will tell you it is full. Ignore this, for it rarely is, and push note two across the counter: 'I am a student, and I want to pay student prices.'

Support this if possible with an International Student ID card, which any Chinese official will regard with grave mistrust. At this stage, you have basically overcome the first directive, the question of luxury, and are starting on the second, the question of price.

For any bed, there will be at least seven different prices which the official can apply. The list, in descending order, goes something like this:

Foreign guest (tourist)
Foreign student
Foreign expert
Chinese overseas student (Taiwanese)
Chinese
Chinese student
Chinese official

Unfortunately the category of foreign student is not yet established. The furtherance of this category is something every budget traveller struggles to achieve. We call it 'educating the officials in the correct line'. It is always vital to find out whether an official has been educated or not. Some of them take much longer to teach than others. It can be a matter of two hours if you are pioneering a route. It is just a question of sticking to your guns and remaining polite. If you raise your voice you might as well give up. The other thing to remember is that the official has no direct personal interest in the amount you pay. It will not affect him or his salary, for these hotels are run by the state. It is just a question of persuading him that what he is doing is good policy. If you can show him other hotel receipts so that he realises that it is established procedure, and that he isn't setting a precedent, he will normally come round. It says something for the flexibility of the people and the system that this is possible. The consequent drop in price is dramatic. Travellers who are surprised at this have misunderstood the basics of what has been happening. You have not been bargaining. Everything has a fixed price. You have merely been discussing which regulation to apply to your situation. You do not say:

'I'll give you two pounds.'
'I'm sorry, sir, the price is twenty pounds.'
'All right, then, five pounds.'
'Perhaps fifteen pounds?'
'Ten pounds?'
'Done.'

That is not the scenario at all. You say:

'Two pounds.'
'Twenty pounds.'
'Two pounds.'
'Twenty pounds.'

'Two pounds,' and so on for two hours, until he suddenly sees the force of your argument and agrees on two pounds. Thereafter he can be regarded as at least semi-educated. Of course you are conducting the whole affair from a position of weakness. If you don't win, there is nowhere else you can go. Sleeping in the open is out of the question. Quite apart from the cold, there's nowhere for you to go and the people would not allow it. China Travel Service would be summoned, you would be escorted to your hotel for a night at £20, and perhaps out of the country on the following day. If you lost the battle, you left town the next day anyway, if your luck didn't change. This happens to some people. It only needs one such night to break your budget. Thus China can be the cheapest or most expensive, hardest or easiest country you've ever travelled in. Everywhere you are met with kindness and honesty. It is just a question of learning to play the system.

We were not to know this on our first day, trudging, shoulders hunched against the wind, through the blue masses in huge Canton Square. After our false start at the post office we eventually manage to find the hotel. Fortunately other travellers have blazed a trail here, and we get cheap dormitory beds after only two minutes.

'Wow, this hotel is something else,' says John, as a smiling Chinese receptionist shows us down long warm corridors to our dormitory. Each bed has a heavy cotton quilt on it, twice the weight and warmth of a Western duvet. These are used all over China. The people spin them like candy floss or huge white spider webs.

This is my introduction to one of China's most important and universal products: cotton. Without cotton life in China would be impossible. There are two things for which the government provides coupons: food and cotton. These are the basics of life over here, and everyone must get a certain minimum, but despite the abundance of cotton, I never once saw it growing in the south.

Outside our window are parked the two hotel taxis for the use of foreigners and officials. These are marvellous machines with blunt noses and wide running boards, straight out of a thirties gangster movie, but, far from being veteran, they are brand-new. It is only the design which is antique. Apparently the Russians spent twenty years copying it from the Americans, before the Chinese spent a further twenty copying it from the Russians. As far as they're concerned, it's the latest thing.

The same lesson is to be seen all around. Valve radios, valve televisions, steam irons, steam engines, hand pumps, hand carts, all the products which the West abandoned years ago, are rolled out, spanking new off the production line. Certainly these things are still in existence elsewhere, but nowhere are they manufactured on the same scale as here.

Night falls and we go around the corner to a local restaurant. What a contrast this makes to Hong Kong. What a contrast to any other town I've been in. It has streets and houses like a Western town, yet it's as strange to me as any mud hut society.

China's fascination lies in the fact that it offers a viable alternative way of life. This is not a second-rate imitation of Western society.

At 6.30 p.m. the streets still hum with activity; it is the sound of people that fills the air. The occasional light shines out from a shop or restaurant. The Chinese regard electricity as a precious commodity and use it sparingly; its silent force is still a source of wonder to them.

We go into the restaurant, a haven of light and warmth in the darkness. Chinamen crowd round tables in the cheery yellow glow, silently delighted to see us in their restaurant. The cook shows us great cauldrons of soup, stew and rice, stacked round with bowls and chopsticks. We point to what we want, and attempt to pay, but are motioned over to a desk by the door. Here a lady sells a selection of coloured tickets. We've no idea what simmers in the cauldrons, or what each ticket signifies, but we point to what we think we want, hand over some money, and hope for the best. All restaurants are run on this ticket system. Often the tickets and the food are at different ends of the room, with long queues leading up to each. Buying blind is not a good idea since you're likely to end up with two bowls of rice and an egg. You must either point to what someone else is having at a nearby table, or buy the same ticket as the person in front of you. This adds an extra element of chance to your meal. You're never sure what you are getting till it's in front of you, and sometimes not even then. The Chinese are a remarkably omnivorous race. There is a saying: if it flies and it's not a plane, if it floats and it's not a boat, if it moves and it's not a bicycle, the Cantonese will eat it.

I end up with a bowl of soup the size of a bird-bath, an equally enormous bowl of rice, and a plate of meat and vegetables. With some difficulty I drain the steaming bowl of soup, but before I can embark upon the next course, it is whipped away and replaced by another bowl of equally colossal dimensions. The cook smiles encouragingly at me.

'What am I going to do, John?' I say, 'There's no way I'm going to get through this.'

'Well, you can't hurt her feelings,' he replies helpfully, 'you'll just have to finish it.'

With a supreme effort I get to the bottom of the bowl once

more, but again, before I can move, another appears in its place.

'It's no good, I'll have to start on the rice or I'll never get to the end of the meal.'

So saying, I take a token sip of my soup, and wielding my chopsticks with what I hope passes for casual mastery, start shovelling down my rice like everyone else. This must be more hygienic than using fingers and more efficient than using a knife and fork. Perhaps that, together with the fact that they only drink boiled water, explains why Chinese are healthier than Indians. If you've got to boil your water, it's no extra trouble to drop in a few herbal leaves to make it taste good; this has helped the popularity of tea in China. There's a tremendous range on offer, anything from thick brown clods which look and taste like camel dung, to aromatic petals and flowers producing delicate scented brews. For the humbler, plain hot water must suffice. Boring as it may sound, even this seems to take on a distinctive flavour in China.

There's no doubt that the implement you use to eat your food affects the way it tastes, and to my mind wood in the mouth is better than metal. Chopsticks are easy to wash too. I watch them steaming in the tub beside me like a heap of swollen matchsticks. When chopsticks are to be used the food must be cut up into bite-sized portions before cooking. For a people whose staple diet is rice, however, this doesn't present too much of a problem. All goes well till I'm given a bowl of greasy peanuts to eat. Having deftly transferred half the contents from my bowl to the floor, I resort to a more primitive and less hygienic way of eating.

Chinamen seated at tables round about gaily call for more rice. I don't know how they manage it. Never have I seen such small people eat such large helpings. Yet they rarely become fat. Unlike their compatriots abroad, with their reputation for rotundity and pigeon toes, these people are well-built, with just that touch of bow-leggedness which characterises the Oriental.

Now I know why Chinese chopsticks are so long. It's so that they can reach across at the communal meal to the delicious dishes on the far side of the table. There's no question of passing things round here; it's a matter of helping yourself. Watching them all tuck in makes me think of the Chinese parable of the hree gluttons in hell. Because of their outstanding greed on earth, the three gluttons were condemned to sit around a small able in hell, piled high with food, armed with chopsticks that vere just too long for them. So intent were they in their fruitless efforts to feed their own faces, that they never thought to feed each other, and so they remained, perpetually struggling, yet perpetually hungry. Not of course that these Chinese have any difficulty in feeding themselves (the only person who suffers from that problem is myself). They seem to be holding a competition to see who can eat the most the quickest. Unless you're pretty snappy with the chopsticks you could starve to death around here. Despite this fine example, my third bowl of soup defeats me. I stagger off, soup swilling around inside me, guiltily leaving a half-empty bowl on the table. Thus was I introduced to an old Cantonese custom. If you finish your soup before starting the next course, it is a sign that you are still hungry and want some more. If you ever want to get to the end of your meal, leave a little in the bottom of the bowl. I learnt my lesson that night.

The next day we look for the Public Security Office to get our travel visas and find it next to a building site. Dozens of Chinese eat into the hillside with pick-axes and buckets, like an army of worker ants. Bamboo scaffolding and red bricks lie in neat piles. Everywhere in Canton you see people building. This is a showpiece city. As the setting for China's biannual trade fair it is the city by which overseas investors will judge China. Forty-five years ago it was a fever-infested slum settlement. Now it has broad streets and brick buildings. Not so interesting, one might be forgiven for suggesting, as old wooden Chinatown, but not so squalid to live in either. It is still possible to find the higgledy-piggledy charm of old China, with its interlocking roofs and lattice of guttering, but you must look for it down the side streets. The main roads, covering Canton with a tarmac grid, are more like motorways, the outside lanes packed full of bicyclists, the inside ones empty but for the occasional tram rumbling by with its overhead lines. Such facilities in a country which decries cars as materialistic, may seem a little surprising, yet China has always planned its towns in this manner. Traditionally, broad north/south, east/west streets, carefully aligned on the points of the compass, split up the community into islands. Within these, narrow alleys or *hutong* wind hither and thither. Thus was formed almost a series of villages within the city walls. Outside town, broad bridges stand deserted in the fields. Little country lanes lead on to these incongruously huge structures, while a stream trickles timidly underneath, embarrassed at all the trouble it has caused, but it needn't worry for no one comes this way. The creaking wheels of a hand-drawn cart are all that disturbs the rustic quiet.

The inspiration behind the large-scale industrial planning is to be found not in China, but further to the north in the Soviet Union. After the Second World War, the Soviets tried to guide China along the way to heavy industry, but the Chinese saw where that path led. They had no wish to create the sort of clanking war machine that held the Soviet Union in thrall, consuming the flower of the nation in its metal jaws and condemning the rest to starve in the fields. They turned their back on Russia and its ways, and pursued their own path to agrarian prosperity. They realised that their primary aim must be to feed and clothe the nation. Only then could China set about building an economy, and then only slowly, by encouraging indigenous domestic industry. The headlong pursuit of high technology heavy industry would only give rise to an unbalanced economy; this, sooner or later, would come crashing down on the heads of its makers, unless propped up by foreign aid applied by foreign men with foreign ways.

The Chinese read Karl Marx. They knew economic forces turned the wheels of history, and they knew that if the Soviets turned the wheels of their economy, the Soviets would rule their land. This was economic imperialism: more insidious but no less effective than the military sort. Rifts in ideology became more and more apparent and the Soviets less and less prepared to paper them over for the sake of a united Communist front. Relations deteriorated until 1960 when the Russians reneged on all their contracts and walked out of the country. Relations reverted to the more traditional state of animosity. China had once again to look to its Great Wall for protection. China renounced its 'left mistakes' and set about developing its own economy in its own way. Now Russia is removing nuclear missiles from its western frontier and redeploying them in the east. It recognises its enemy.

The Chinese are a patient and resilient people. For the sake of their independence they will go through all the stages from light to heavy industry. They will make mistakes, but at least they will be their own mistakes. The Chinese continue to build roads and apartment blocks as before, but they use men, not machines. With a population of one billion they have little need for labour-saving equipment or heavy plant. Bamboo scaffolding holds up their houses quite as well as tubular steel does ours. Why import scaffolding when you can grow your own? The Chinese seek a natural economy suitable for the means and needs of their nation. They do not wish to import foreign ways and wants. They seek to learn from, but not to rely on, the West. I admire them for their independence, their perseverance and their refusal to take short cuts.

The economies of Europe are controlled by market forces, and that of China by the State, but the two systems are not so far apart as we may imagine. The West, on the whole, has come down in favour of capitalism and competition, tempered by taxation and social welfare. The People's Republic has chosen Communism and cooperation, tempered now by 'individual economy'. Starting from opposite points the two are moving together. China has had to abandon its old ethic 'from each according to his means, to each according to his needs', and replace it with a new one, 'from each according to his means, to each according to his work'. In some ways it can be even harsher than the West: 'he who does not work, neither shall he eat.' The profit element has returned to Chinese society, incentive has returned, and production increased. Free markets are springing up. Even so far as salaries paid by the state are concerned, inequalities have crept in. There is an eight-point scale of financial remuneration based on contribution to the national interest and varying from peasants and factory workers (the vast majority) at the bottom, to high-level government officials at the top.

There is a delicate balance in China between the ideas of liberty and equality. Under Mao the scales stood firmly in favour of equality. Anyone attempting to tip them in favour of individual liberty was likely to fall further than he expected. But now as the problems of poverty begin to prevail over those of liberty, and the economy over those of political philosophy, the balance is tipping back towards freedom. The Maoists are fearful as they see their old leader's ideas being overturned. They criticise the new leader, Deng Xiao Ping, for introducing capitalism, and indeed a wave of materialism has hit the nation, but he at least can turn to his critics and say, 'Well, it works,' an answer Mao was never able to give. A man fighting for a cause is willing to endure physical deprivation, for his mind is consumed by an ideal. The cause over, his mind naturally turns to his material surroundings. A nation cannot be fighting permanently for a cause. Now the revolution is over, the Chinese must find a new direction for their energies.

Despite this, the ideal of equality is fundamental to the People's Republic. It must be admitted that workers in the towns are materially better off than their peasant brothers in the fields, and important politicians are better off than workers in the factory. There are murmurs about the formation of a bureaucratic élite, cruising around in taxis, staying in special hotels and using special shops. To a certain extent this is happening. To a certain extent it is inevitable under this system, but it could be worse.

The most powerful man in China, Mao, maintained his simple habits to the end, sleeping on a straw mattress, and wearing his famous Mao suits. This suit is something of a misnomer, for in truth, Dr Sun Yat Sen was the first to popularise it, though I suppose a 'Sun Yat Sen Suit' doesn't have quite the same ring to it.

Clothes can have a great levelling effect on people. The members of a rugby team, or a school, or a prison, all wear the same clothes as an outward and visible sign that they are part of the same group and treated in the same way. No distinction is made between them. Mao did the same for China, he put the people into uniform. There were no special cases. Ostentatious clothing could be socially divisive.

This idea has been taken to a ludicrous extreme in the Chinese army, where official rank has been abolished. Every soldier wears the same clothes and there is no insignia, though apparently officers are distinguished by the fact that they have four pockets instead of two. This is surprising. The whole point of insignia or uniforms is to signify a chain of command so that soldiers can tell at a glance who their commanding officer is.

In wartime this could be vital and it is ridiculous to pretend that there is no distinction between the commanders and the commanded. I put the problem to a Chinese soldier, and he answered it to his complete satisfaction by telling me that their rank was sewn to the inside of their caps where no one can see it. I can't help but imagine a group of Chinese soldiers doffing their hats to each other in a gentlemanly fashion while the bombs fall all around.

Once again, however, Mao forgot to take account of the human element in his plans. Humans are individuals. They have their own features and personalities. They are not identical. If they were they would be machines. Staff officials wear badges for identification but on the badges are written numbers, not names. Humans resent being treated as if they were mere numbers. Schoolboys and prisoners resent uniforms. They cannot wait to assert their individuality by changing into their own clothes. I think the same is true of the Chinese. Fashion, in places such as Shanghai and Peking, is making a tentative come-back. People are still scared to dress up (that could be interpreted as bourgeois) but they are bored with Mao suits. Pierre Cardin has already paid a visit to Peking. Changes are on the way and the government now even allows Western-style suits to be sold in some shops.

The Party carries its campaign for uniformity to an extreme length. It seems that it would like everyone to be equal in every respect: even physically. It would like a nation of conformists. It discourages beauty. Pretty women, far from making the most of themselves, attempt to hide their beauty. There are more important things to be in the People's Republic, than beautiful. The individual should sacrifice himself to the state. Only thus can he achieve immortality, for while the individual will die, the state will live for ever. In this, however, the Party will never succeed, unless it can indeed produce a race of clones. Man by his nature, by his very being, is an individual. If he loses his individuality, he loses his humanity. This would be the ultimate victory of equality over freedom.

We enter the offices of the Public Security Bureau, Gonganju or police. Far from the vaguely threatening sinister figure we had expected, a cheery old tea-lady greets us at the desk. She bustles out and fetches a young man dressed in the inevitable blue uniform. Only his shiny leather Shanghai shoes and wrist watch reveal him as being a member of the élite.

The Chinese police are feared. They are the arm of central government stretching out over the people, the hand which everyone fears will grasp them by the shoulder, the ear which makes everyone think twice before speaking. They are the 'thought' police. It is no longer necessary to commit a counter-revolutionary action, just to think it may be enough. Though not apparent, the police are pervasive. The Chinese have carried the idea of a 'plain-clothes policemen' as far as it can possibly go: everyone wears plain clothes. It is inevitable that enforcers of justice in a totalitarian régime, where all criticism is seen as treason, should be unpopular. They can be harsh and devious but they have never plumbed the depths of the KGB. They are just doing their job and upholding the will of the republic, and isn't that what all good Communists should be doing anyway? If the state is not perfect, as they are led to believe, well, it isn't their fault. Better bad government than anarchy, better anarchy than capitalist thraldom.

Perhaps because they are not the final power in the land, they lack the overweaning arrogance necessary to commit the atrocities that come so naturally to police states. Ultimate power in China rests with the army, and it is a people's army. Although Mao did much to confuse and hence discredit the Gonganju, it was the Red Brigades and not the police or army, that were responsible for the horror of the Cultural Revolution. Thus the officer can find it in his soul to share a smile with us, though he speaks few words of English. We try to obtain from him a list of places which we are permitted to visit, but without success. This is obviously 'classified' information. Though the Chinese authorities have apparently designated a hundred places as being open to visitors I suspect that, if a Western eye was allowed to gaze upon it, the list would appear somewhat shorter than it does to the Oriental. As it is, we point on our map to the places that we wish to visit, and say the name boldly while he writes it down. This is not as simple as it may sound since the old Wade-Giles spelling used on our English maps has now been replaced by Pinyin. Peking has become Beijing, Nanking – Nanjing, Tientsing – Tianjin, Xian – Sian, Kweilin – Guilin and Canton – Guangzhou.

As we leave the Bureau an unfortunate incident occurs that gives us an insight into the way the Chinese treat each other and their guests. A man was standing on top of an old trestle stepladder cleaning the ceiling. As we pass, the frayed rope holding the two legs of the ladder together snaps, the ladder collapses like a giraffe doing the splits and down tumbles the man to daze himself on the hard flagstones beneath. Before we can move, half a dozen Chinese have appeared from nowhere, picked up the stunned man, and bundled him out of the hall. The incident is over in a minute and the hall back to its previous calm. The young officer stands quietly behind his desk as if nothing had happened. I am amazed at the speed and efficiency of the operation and yet saddened. The man was not whisked off for his own sake, but for ours. Such incidents are not for Western eyes. In China accidents do not occur. I have a feeling the worker disgraced himself.

Next to the Public Security Bureau is a bakery. Bakeries are a welcome and surprising feature of Chinese towns. Surprising in that they exist, here in the rice-growing south at any rate, and surprising in that they don't bake bread. A large selection of biscuits is what they have to offer. You can buy anything from huge rock bun affairs to tiny wafer tit-bits, but they all share one feature: without exception they taste of sawdust. If the Chinese had set out with the intention of creating the world's most boring biscuit, they could not have done better. Surely it doesn't take much to turn a bad biscuit into a good one? Is the Oriental sense of taste so different from our own or are the people just putting a brave face on it and making a virtue of necessity? After an extensive survey of the goods on offer, we find one type of biscuit which is almost edible and confine ourselves to that for the rest of the trip. It is still made of sawdust, but of a slightly higher quality wood than the rest.

We stroll around town while our visas are being prepared, passing through the park and down to the river. Some fine old buildings line the waterfront. Broad porches with overhanging upper storeys provide a sheltered colonnade for pedestrians. These were the homes of the European traders in the days when Canton was a treaty port. Now they are bustling Chinese shops. Huge hinged trams, packed to the gunwales, crawl along the roads like articulated caterpillars, blue sparks hissing and crackling from their antiquated powerlines. There are no street hawkers here. There's no room for them. The pavement is a solid mass of blue. All the wares are carefully stored and priced in the shops, ordered and regulated like the rest of Chinese society; sorted, packaged, labelled and stacked in blocks one on top of the other, like the people living in the town.

Perhaps this is not such a bad thing. Consider the alternatives. The blocks are clean; so are the people. The prices are fixed; the people can afford them. If you go to a shop in India to buy an apple you will wait an age while Indians push and shove in front of you. When you have at last fought your way through to the front of the queue, the owner will ignore you while he serves his friends behind you. You eventually catch his attention, he gives you the worst apple he can find because you are a fool and don't know his ways. He charges twice what it should cost. People shout at you to hurry up. You give up the battle, reach for your wallet, and discover that it's been stolen. Later on, you are glad you never managed to get an apple, since your friend who did has been ill for a week as a result. In China the people themselves will take you to the front of the queue where the owner will proudly pick out the best fruit he has and present it to you, and you can be sure you will pay the same price for it as the man behind you.

Canton has a few gastronomic surprises to offer. Along with the pig's carcasses and occasional chickens hanging up on hooks, you can see skinned dogs, appallingly naked without their fur, dangling by a hind leg. They're very popular in China. Apparently they taste like chicken but have the consistency of tongue, depending on the breed of course. So many Chinese have been so hungry for so long, they have grown used to eating almost anything. The more inedible a thing appears, the more of a delicacy the Chinese pretend it to be. Although tree bark no longer appears on the menu, chicken's head and bull's penis are still considered great delicacies. Mrs Thatcher drank sea-slug soup on her recent visit to Peking, and bird's nest soup has spread to the West. The Chinese certainly don't suffer from the culinary qualms of their Hindu neighbours.

Further back, the twin spires of what looks like a neo-Gothic cathedral rise above the roof-tops. We go in search of it and find a church a little way inland, grimy and broken but unmistakably Christian, amidst the warehouses. Wooden boxes peep out from the broken slats high in the belfry. Sacks are piled behind the cobwebbed gloom of the stained glass window; a wrought-iron fence surrounds it. We try the gate and a gnarled old caretaker appears like a disfigured genie. He produces an enormous key, slides it into the lock and turns it. To my surprise the rockers slide back with a sweetly oiled click and the gate swings soundlessly open on its hinges. He beckons us in, a figure from Victor Hugo, but as soon as a local approaches, he shouts at him furiously and slams the gate to. For the first, but not the last time, a shiver of indignation runs down my vertebrae, not because the man had not been admitted, but because we have. Uncomfortable to go on, yet hesitant to go back for fear of seeming churlish, I climb the steps to the church door.

This one groans as I expected. Inside are boxes – stacks of boxes: boxes in the nave, boxes in the transept, boxes in the tower, boxes in the crypt, boxes where the pews should be, boxes where the bishop should be, boxes where the people should be, boxes where the shrine should be and there, just where the altar should be – a cross. If the boxes are extraordinary, the cross is ten times more so. Though the church has become a warehouse and the preachers all are dead, the Word lives on, and one brave soul at least exists to speak it. That one rude cross, ugly and bent, means more than all the crucifixes I have ever seen, and it means more to him who made it. This government, that counts religion amongst the five freedoms of its constitution, is the same that burned the temples, closed the churches and even now outlaws the Bible as politically subversive. That cross could be a crucifix yet.

Chastened, we return to the Public Security Bureau to pick up our visas. They are written in Chinese. This time the police officer reads out the names of the places we are allowed to visit while we find them on the map. On leaving, I foolishly enquire about the man who fell.

'What man?' comes the reply.

3

Coolies' Hats on the Landscape: Wuzhou

 MOST PEOPLE travel from Canton to Guilin by train. We want to travel by boat. The two towns are connected by the Xijiang or Pearl River, which passes through some of the loveliest country in China. Beloved by artists, it is the inspiration behind many of the soaring crags and tumbling waterfalls of traditional Chinese art. What better way to see it than from the slow calm of the river? Peace flees the clanking of trains. Unfortunately it is forbidden for foreigners to travel to Guilin by boat. The Public Security Bureau refused us permission to visit Wuzhou, the halfway town. Now we will test the power of the authorities.

We pick up our things and march off to the docks on the river. As ever, long orderly queues stretch back from each little window of the ticket office. We pick a Chinaman and thrust out our little piece of paper saying 'Wuzhou'. This is greeted with much consternation. A crowd gathers, and the paper is passed from hand to hand.

'Wuzhou' we say, helpfully pointing to ourselves. No response. Perhaps they think we are introducing ourselves. We get out some money and point to the queues: 'Wuzhou.'

Immediately one of the crowd, a little quicker or should I say braver than the rest (one is never quite sure whether a Chinaman fails to respond because he doesn't understand or because he is afraid) beckons us to follow him. We march straight to the front of a queue in his wake, to the smiling approval of those in it, hand him some money and, before we know it, have two tickets for Wuzhou. What is more, he hands back nearly all the money which I gave him (probably about a month's wages). I count it out. The tickets come to £1 each, local price, as opposed to the £20, tourist price, demanded by the railways. I would like our helper to keep some of the change, but he refuses. When a Chinaman helps you, he does so out of kindness. To pay would cheapen the gift of friendship bestowed on you. He helps you as an equal.

After all the stories we have heard, we can scarcely believe our good fortune. Our next task is to find out when the boat goes. We get out our invaluable 'what time?' sign. This always seems to create problems. The Chinese system of counting is different from our own. They do it all on one hand. My digital watch from Singapore does not help the situation at all. The safest thing to do is draw a picture of an old-fashioned watch face, and get them to fill in the hands. Though the Chinese have a stubborn tendency to make both hands the same length, and don't always understand the rules, they always enjoy taking part in this game. This man, however, dismisses our attempts to draw a watch as harmless eccentricity and bundles us off to a boat ready and waiting to go. Here he passes us on to a stewardess who takes us to our berth.

We are on an old-fashioned steamer three decks deep, with two layers of bunks along each wall, one at floor level and the other jutting out like a shelf four feet above it. The berths can best be described as long trays, divided up into units by slotted planks. Each person has a unit six and a half feet long by two and a half feet wide – just big enough for a Chinaman and his luggage, but scarcely big enough for a six foot four inch Westerner with size twelve feet. There are no cabins. Cabins are divisive socially as well as physically, and waste space.

We cast off and cruise upstream at surprising speed. At first the landscape is unrelentingly flat and largely industrial, but soon we come amongst fertile farmland. Much of China is harsh and mountainous, so it has had to rely on its river plains for agriculture. These naturally became centres of population and culture. China, as a nation, has evolved around three rivers, the Huangho or Yellow River to the north, the Yangtse in the

centre and the Pearl River to the south. The Pearl is the smalles
of the three, but its broad alluvial delta formed by soil carried
down from the Himalayan mountains hundreds of miles to the
west, make it one of the most fertile areas in China. Heavy
rainfall and tropical heat in all but the winter months enable the
people to grow three rice crops a year. Further upstream are
fruit and mulberry trees. The latter are used for feeding the
worms from whose tiny jaws comes the much-prized shiny silk
thread. Europeans in days gone by believed silk grew on trees.
They were not so far wrong. Silk worms live on mulberry leaves

The occasional tiered tower, like a stack of coolies' hats,
breaks the horizon. Largely derelict now, these were lookout
posts of old. One, more substantial than the rest, seems to have
been restored to its former use.

The galley at the back of the boat starts turning out bowls of
cabbage soup and noodles but, before we get any, a stewardess
comes to fetch us. We follow her up through the decks to the
very roof of the steamer. Here, beaming with delight, stands the
captain. He has prepared a feast on top of his boat. A wooden
table stands covered in dishes. He bows to us. I, to his surprise
step forward, and shake him by the hand, not perhaps a very
hygienic custom for an agrarian community, but with so many
customs for me to learn, I might as well introduce one or two
myself. We take our seats like guests at the mad hatter's tea
party, and, with the wind whistling through the dishes, snatch-
ing the carelessly angled spoonful of soup from under the nose of
the unwary diner, begin our feast. A bottle of Shanghai beer is
produced, ceremoniously drunk, and replaced. Water washed
down from the Himalayas passes us on its journey to the South
China Sea. China unrolls before us, as we stand to toast the
Queen, the President and the Chairman. The meal eaten, and
honour done to all our nations, we return to our bunks and are
lulled to sleep by the womblike throb of the ship's engines.

Dawn breaks pink above the hills. The steamer shimmers
through an early morning mist. The hills draw back and we
enter a drowned valley filled with cloud and water. We steam
on. The mist lifts to reveal Wuzhou in a crook of the river. The
steamer docks and our trials begin anew.

John and I are carried ashore with the crowd and deposited
on the steps of the harbour offices. A wizened old man, all

curves, with bow legs, arched back, and moon face, comes up to us. 'Follow me,' he signals, and we do, around the corner of the building to some offices on the far side. Oh, dear, this looks like the Public Security Bureau: 'Visas please.'

We hand them over.

No Wuzhou. Dear me. Much pointing of fingers and wagging of heads. Now that these foreigners are here, something must be done with them. Why do foreigners put us in this difficult position?

Two slips of paper are covered in Chinese characters and handed over to us. What can they mean? I point to the steamer on the river. No, not that. John does a very passable imitation of a coach equipped with a loud horn. Yes, that.

'What time?' Our invaluable piece of paper comes to our assistance. The officials apparently go to sleep.

'We sleep here?'

'Yes. Good.'

That settled, our self-appointed guide takes us off to the square and climbs into a rickshaw bolted to the back of an ancient motorbike. The rider kicks it into action, races through the gears, and hits a top speed of 10 m.p.h. Wind-assisted, we cruise along the road and pass over an enormous bridge spanning a tributary of the Pearl River. Covered barges crowd the banks like a log jam in the lumber season. We head for a bluff on the far side upon which stands a large grey building: the hotel.

More officials take us to our room. Our 'guide', less at home here, hovers nervously by the door, clutching his pipe. John seizes the opportunity to press some of his American tobacco on him and sends him steaming happily off home. The hotel is big, stark and Soviet. There is no heating and no sitting-room. A door opens from our room to a small balcony above the river. Extraordinarily, it has great vents cut in it through which whistles a chill wind fresh from the Himalayas. Bare, cold and box-like as it is, it would be a palace compared to a Chinaman's home. No wonder the Chinese spend their leisure time in the streets and the parks. There is nowhere else for them to go.

Wuzhou was a flourishing port in the last century, receiving many British ships from nearby Hong Kong. Sadly it was devastated a mere ten years ago during the Cultural Revolution when rival Red Brigades clashed in the town centre. The losing side claimed 50,000 of its men had died – greater casualties than the Americans suffered in the whole of the Vietnam War. Thus much of the town today is rather cold and modern.

One thing which distinguishes a Chinese crowd from crowds elsewhere is its sense of purpose. The streets are always full of people walking in a determined manner, as if they are just slightly late for a pressing engagement but don't want to appear to be in a hurry. At first I was amazed at the activity, and thought I must have hit town at some sort of rush hour, but watching from my balcony as the day wears on, the crowd shows no signs of diminishing. It dawns on me that this is a permanent state of affairs. People are not hurrying to work, in fact I don't think they are hurrying anywhere. They are jaywalking like any other nation, only they're slightly better at disguising the fact. It's a law of physics, I suppose: cram a lot of people into a little space, and that space is always going to be full. It's a fact of life here that towns are large, not in area, but in population. You scarcely feature on the map unless you are over a million strong. Shanghai, one of the biggest cities in the world at 14 million, is just another town in China.

I wonder if this crowding worries them. I think every Englishman's dream is to have a house in the country. I don't think the Orientals share this dream. An Englishman's home is his castle – a Chinaman's is, perhaps, his commune. A friend of mine at home was involved in settling Vietnamese boat-people in northern England. He put families into rooms in an apartment block when they arrived. On visiting them the next day he found them all hopelessly crammed into one room. They didn't want a place of their own. To them numbers spell strength and security. In China, three generations may live in the same room. Privacy is a commodity the people do without.

The Chinese have protected Westerners by passing a regulation forbidding anyone other than foreigners, and, of course, politicians, from entering tourist hotels. This can come as an unpleasant surprise if you are not ready for it. You may have made friends with a Chinaman and be communicating with him, only to find that he is turned back at the gates of your hotel. Nothing you can say will make any difference. You will be treated with the utmost deference, and he with contempt. You can only stand by helplessly and watch. Our self-appointed guide of this morning knew this better than we. You are told, of course, that the regulation exists only for your own good, and to an extent this is true. The Chinese are inquisitive by nature. Given the opportunity, half the population of town would wander in to see what you looked like but that is not the real reason behind the rule. The primary motive is to stop Chinese from associating with foreigners. The authorities fear that exposure to the West will make the people dissatisfied with their lot. A little knowledge can be a dangerous thing. The people are warned not to speak to foreigners, lest they be 'contaminated', yet they are encouraged to learn English. They must communicate with the West in order to learn from it, but this does not mean they wish to adopt Western values. All students at university learn a foreign language. Government posts above a certain level are open only to those who can speak English, but at the same time the authorities warn their students to keep away from their teachers. The segregation is worse now than it has ever been. The 'old school' of revolutionary thought will not allow the spread of Western values. This would be a betrayal of everything they had fought for in the Revolution. Inevitably such a policy breeds resentment amongst visitors and teachers. They feel that they are being used and that China is merely out for what it can get.

It is very easy for a Westerner coming into China to criticise, but all he sees is China as it is today. He can have little idea of China as it was before, or whether the present is an improvement on the past. This is the comparison which should be made. The easy comparison between China as it is today and the West as it is today can be obvious and unfair. It is less what China is than what it is becoming that is important, and the same, of course, must be said of the West. It is both easy and wrong for the West to adopt a paternalistic attitude to the East. The East has different immediate problems and may find different immediate solutions. The East has a different approach to the problems of humanity. East can learn from West, and West from East. Perhaps our final solution will be the same.

The two most immediate problems that any Westerner must see in China are poverty and lack of freedom. In the idea of liberty and its mirror-image, service, lies perhaps the most fundamental divergence of belief between China and the West. China has always valued service. In the past it has practised the Confucian virtue of service to the Emperor; today it professes the Communist virtue of service to the state. The West has always valued individual freedom and self-determination. This, perhaps, is a difference between Communism and capitalism, between working for others and working for yourself. It is hard to tell in which activity true freedom lies. It is possible to be a slave to yourself as surely as to be a slave to anyone else. Abraham Lincoln remarked, 'Freedom to the lamb may mean the right to live undisturbed, whilst freedom to the wolf may mean the right to eat the lamb.'

What, then, does freedom mean to the Chinese today? In practical terms, as laid down in their constitution, it means the five guarantees: a job, a place to live, an education, a medical service, a burial. Westerners may find this a strange definition of freedom but it does make an important point. No man is free in any practical sense of the word unless he enjoys a certain basic standard of living. The impoverished man, fighting to survive, is a slave to his environment. He may be free from certain things (restrictions) but he is not free or able to do other things (capabilities). The West may now take this for granted. The Chinese cannot, hence the five guarantees, hence the tremendous emphasis on developing the economy, even, perhaps at the expense of their Communist philosophy. Where the problems of poverty and doctrine come into conflict, the former now takes priority. In the days of the Cultural Revolution the opposite was true and, as a result, poverty ruled. A veteran worker is quoted as saying: 'My son does not have to make the agonising decision of his ancestors to drown an infant because it is an extra mouth to feed, to sell a child as a servant to the landlord, or to rely on a teenage daughter forced into prostitution.' These are not the sort of choices Chinese want to have to make. Thus the problem of freedom is tied up with the problem of poverty.

The March 1978 constitution defines freedom as 'the right to own a home, to provide and claim an inheritance, to strike, to practise religion or atheism, and to register a complaint against an elected or appointed official without fear of reprisal.' Though the last three 'freedoms' might be considered more professed than real, they do at least reveal an ideal. The reality is that the Chinese people are so hedged around with rules and regulations that they are afraid to do anything themselves. Initiative is stifled. Life is the constant consideration of 'what is permitted', and the entity which tells them what they should be doing is the State.

The West works from a different premise: a premise of natural freedom, assuming that you can do something unless it is expressly forbidden by the state. You are free from restrictions. This freedom is a natural thing and is something you are born with. It is not something given to you by the state. Ideally, we believe in 'life, liberty, and the pursuit of happiness'. We believe in self-determination. Perhaps this is an idea more accessible to a Christian culture than to one imbued traditionally with the Buddhist principle of the circle of life.

The Eastern and Western approaches to freedom are thus diametrically opposed. Perhaps the Eastern approach with its emphasis on the communal rather than the individual, recognising the inherent authority of the community, is more logical. Only a man living on his own can really be free. We should be slow to criticise the Chinese for lacking something they do not necessarily believe in, and be aware, at least, of the alternative approach.

This is the obvious comparison between the concept of freedom in the West and in the East. The more important question, having gauged how free the Chinese are, is whether they are freer today than they were before. Or to put it another way, whether Chinese society is becoming more free. The Chinese today are not free to marry until the age of twenty-five as men or twenty-three as women; they are not free to have more than one child; they are not free to choose their own jobs; they are not free to live where they want; they are not free to leave the country; they are not free to buy what they want; they are not free to read what they want; they are not free to say what they want. Some Chinese do not expect such freedom, and accept state regulation. Many are grateful, because in some ways they are better off than they were before. Marriage had always been a matter at least of parental consent, jobs and housing a question of economic necessity, travel impossible, and criticism of the Emperor or feudal landlord unthinkable. Today, people may be told

where to live, but at least they have a roof over their head; the
may be told what to do, but at least they have a job; they ma
not be able to buy what they want, but at least they won'
starve; they may not be able to read what they want, but at leas
they will be able to read. These immense achievements affect
ing a quarter of the world's population are the result of massiv
state regulation. Given the chaotic state of the nation in 1949
the vastness of its area, and the poorness of its communications
they could have been achieved in no other way. The Chinese ar
winning their battle against poverty and their achievement
could only be gained by force. Mao supplied that force. Inevit
ably, when force is used people get hurt. Unquestionably ther
is much resentment and still a long way to go, but there coul
have been more hurt and more resentment if no force had bee
used.

There is little to hold us in the hotel, so we walk to the top of th
nearby hill. To our surprise, we find an open air theatre cut int
the crest. With the Pearl River for a backdrop and trees for
wall, this is a superb setting. It is obviously in use too, probabl
for opera, China's favourite form of entertainment. We follow
path down the hill, across the bridge, and into town, I to find
barber, and John to take some photographs. Unfortunately n
one will cut my locks (perhaps they are too astonished at thei
colour), so I return to the hotel.

No sooner have I gone into my room than there is a knock o
the door.

'Come in,' is my automatic response. There is no reaction
course.

I open the door to find the hotel clerk and another ma
standing outside in the corridor.

'Please can we come in?'

'Yes, do.'

They shuffle in looking embarrassed.

'My friend and I would like to talk with you.'

'Fine.'

There follows a slightly awkward silence until I realise that
is incumbent upon me to say something.

'Your English is very good.'

He breaks into a smile. I have obviously said the right thing.

'No, no, not good,' he says, obviously very proud of himself.

'Yes, it is very good. How long have you been learning?'

'My friend and I have learnt for two years in the evenings, and from BBC World Service and Voice of America, but our English is very poor. This is the first time we speak to English man.'

Such exchanges of pleasantries are a vital start to any conversation in China. Hardly anyone in the south can speak English, but there is an increasing awareness of its importance among the people and a determination to learn. Children are beginning to be taught English at school now. It is still at a rudimentary stage however, and the brighter ones who may need English for their career have to pick up what they can from the radio. Formerly Chinese propaganda dominated the airwaves and it was forbidden to listen to foreign programmes, but that has changed now. In fact the authorities actually broadcast an English language programme on television. For months Katherine Flower would appear on television every evening at 6 p.m. to talk to the nation. There is every reason to believe that she is the most popular Englishwoman who has ever lived. Everyone in China loves her and assumes that you are personally acquainted with her. The first thing they say when they find out that you are English is: 'You must know Katherine Flower.'

If you disappoint them in that, they will produce the only foreign name they can remember: 'Well, perhaps you are friends with Richard Nixon.' Nixon, as the first American President to break the ice and visit Peking in 1972, is a great folk hero in China. Without doubt he is far more popular in China than in the United States. The fact that the width of the Atlantic has always separated you from Richard Nixon does not worry them in the slightest. So far as they are concerned there is only China and the rest of the world. No other distinctions need be drawn.

Although one still feels that about as many Chinese speak English in China as Englishmen speak Chinese in England, the situation is improving. If you visit a town of a couple of million people you will probably find a handful of people who speak English. Word travels fast, they will soon know you've arrived and will try to find you, but as they are not allowed in tourist hotels and are too nervous to eat or drink with you there are problems; after all, they are not supposed to consort with foreigners. It doesn't do to take chances. You never know who may be watching, or what the next régime may say. Best to keep your head down unless you want to become next year's scape-goat. Any verbal exchange is normally limited to a few haltingly delivered, but no doubt endlessly practised, sentences in the street. The deliverer, at the end of his repertoire, and overcome with embarrassment, gives you a carefully prepared 'Thank you' and flees.

Fresh from Hong Kong, on my third day in China, I did not realise the significance of a meeting such as this one. We go on to my balcony and look out over the town.

'What are those pagodas on the hill over there?' I ask.

'That is the town zoo and park.'

'Oh, what animals do you have?'

'We have lion and camel and monkey. Do you want to see them?'

'Yes, thank you.'

'But we must go quickly. Do you ride a bicycle?'

'Yes.'

This causes much consternation. They have a hurried con-versation which ends with the friend shooting off down the corridor. I hope I haven't caused a crisis. Having offered me a bicycle they will move heaven and earth to get one. A bicycle is probably the most prized single possession a Chinaman can have. The manufacturing of bicycles is regulated by the state and each machine carefully licensed. A Chinaman is more proud of his bicycle than any European of his car. It is at least as important as a means of transport and a status symbol. With stereos, washing machines, televisions, furniture, pictures and books, the Westerner's life is so cluttered with possessions that he becomes indifferent to them. If last year's car is slow or out of date, he trades it in for the latest model. This is not the Chinese way. In China, when you buy something you have it for life. There isn't enough to allow wastage. The Chinese are the greatest conservationists in the world. They waste nothing. Nothing is instant, nothing is disposable. In Peking, a full-time staff used to be employed to go through the rubbish of the diplomatic enclave. In Hong Kong I met a team of American scientists preparing to go into China to study techniques of

nergy conservation'. I was never quite sure what this involved
unless it meant staying in bed all day) but they assured me that
he Chinese were world leaders in the field.

An astonishing number of Chinese are involved in repairing
nd recycling: that is why they take such care of their posses-
ons – they build up a lifelong acquaintance with them. A
mashed bowl or broken window is a major disaster. Thus the
an of a bicycle is far from a simple matter. How would you like
lend your treasured car, in which you have invested your life
vings, to a Chinaman who doesn't even know which side of
he road to drive on? By the time we reach the gates, however,
he loan has been organized and my companion's friend awaits
s with three bicycles. Like all other Chinese bicycles they are
eavy, strong, upright and black; the sort of bicycles people
de at home before the war. They are not the flashy lightweight
cers of Europe, or the rusty, ramshackle wrecks of India, but
he sturdy, functional machines of a Communist republic. The
wners seem cast in the same mould, solid and measured. In all
y time in China I didn't see a single accident.

No visit to China is complete without at least one cycling
xpedition. This is mine. Over the bridge and into town we go,
ells blaring in our efforts to get to the zoo in time: the clerk,
ildly daring in the lead, his friend silently disapproving this
arefree abandon, bringing up the rear. There are, of course, no
rs on the road, just streams and streams of bicycles. Rather
ke American commuters, nose to tail, travelling their standard
) mph over the speed limit on the way to work, the Chinese
dal along in lines at a sensible speed, looking askance at the
esponsible elements pushing through on the outside.

I speed through town in the clerk's wake, praying that I
on't have an accident, and ascend the hill on the far side to the
o. Two rather moth-eaten camels, humps keeling over at
usual angles, stare out at us with justifiable ill-humour. Lions
in concrete dens, resolutely refusing to move. A large brown
ar next door steadfastly paces up and down the diagonal of
s cage, determined to get what little exercise he can. I feel
rry for these cramped animals, but then again, their accom-
odation is probably more spacious than their captors'.

Further up we come to the town park or garden. Chinese
rdens are a favourite haunt for old people. Pressure of

employment being what it is, men in China retire at sixty and women at fifty-five. Rather than stay at home, grandad is normally to be found enjoying a pipe with his friends in the garden. But it is not a garden as we would imagine it. It is not natural and green, it is formal and man-made, full of little streams with stepping stones and half-circle bridges, pretty to look at but awkward to walk over. Curious boulders are set into the pavement as natural statues. Pagodas are perched on the hillside as sitting places. We enter one to watch the sun descend to the horizon. Passing behind the bare, gnarled branches of a tree, its face is covered with a shadowy skein of veins. The world is quiet at the magical moment between day and night, until the dark overcomes and the lengthening shadows join to form a single grey.

We pedal back to the hotel for John and dinner. Over our noodles we exchange stories. John found a large playing field on the edge of town, filled with budding football players. Unfortunately there weren't enough footballs to go round, but that didn't matter: tin cans, bundles of rags, anything would do.

Football is a relative newcomer to China. The Chinese are a peaceful race, and on the whole prefer non-contact sports such as badminton and table tennis. Games which don't need much space or equipment are most widespread. Although traditionally strong at table tennis, the Chinese needed a more physical sport with which to establish themselves on the world sporting scene. They found it in volley-ball. They gained their first world championship when their women beat Japan in the 1981 final. The team achieved apotheosis overnight. Here was something of which the Chinese could be proud. Here China led the world. The match is continually being re-run on television. Every Chinese peasant knows the name of every member of that team. They are all national heroines. In the world of football, however, John feels they still have some way to go. While the Chinese system is no doubt capable of producing well coordinated and technically proficient teams, it is unlikely to foster flair and brilliance. The Chinese are trained not to be individuals.

After dinner we go to bed, but with the wind whistling in the bedroom it takes a generous drop of John's Scotch whisky to send us to sleep.

4

The Scenery of Guilin is the Best under Heaven

WE CATCH the early morning bus to Guilin. It's a superb eight-hour trip through the countryside, affording us a rare glimpse of rural China. The rice crop has just been harvested. Curious rocket-shaped haystacks are heaped up out of old rice stalks. The fields are being planted with vegetables in long narrow strips. The peasants fill large butts with water from the low-lying river. In pairs, they drop a bucket suspended on a long loop between them into the water. When they pull the rope taut, the bucket springs up and over, spilling its contents into the butt on the bank. Others fill large watering-cans, sling one over each shoulder and walk down the narrow dividing paths, sprinkling the vegetables as they go. The long perforated spray pipes spread out from their shoulders on either side like bat's wings. In the spring their task becomes easier. The fields here are turned to rice and irrigation channels transport water from the brimming river by force of gravity.

Outside the villages people are making bricks. They choose two fields next to each other, flood the first, turning it into a mud bath, and keep the other dry, so that the sun bakes it hard as rock. They press mud from the wet field into rectangular wooden moulds and turn it out into the dry field to set. When the brick assumes a yellowish tinge, it is ready for use. These seem to be cheap and effective building blocks. Their only drawback is a tendency to crack in half, but then, two small bricks are as good as one large one. All the walls and buildings in the vicinity are made from these bricks, sometimes on their own, sometimes with a layer of mud and straw spread over them to keep the winter chill at bay. I wonder why they don't dissolve in the rainy season? I suppose the soil here has a high clay content.

With their unbroken acquaintance with the land stretching back millennia, the Chinese peasants can always find a natural solution to their problems. While in the West, with greater resources and better communications, any number of solutions to a problem may be available, and, as often as not, an expensive, alien and inappropriate one chosen, in China there is probably only one possible answer; that provided by the land will be the best. These villages made from the earth have a pleasing homogeneity. They blend into the scenery. In every way they are a part of the landscape.

It is strange to find the huge fields in China divided into strips and tended by individuals. Surely here of all places one should see the principles of collectivism put into practice, and the land farmed in communes. Instead, one sees reflected the ancient strip farming system of England in the Middle Ages. The truth is that until Dr Sun Yat Sen overthrew the Imperial Regime in 1911 to found the Republic, China was still in its feudal era, and the peasants using the techniques their ancestors had practised thousands of years earlier. The situation scarcely improved as local warlords dominated the countryside and 'bourgeois elements' gained control of the towns and government. It was not until Mao and his Communists won their long civil war and established the People's Republic of China in 1949, that any real reform could take place, and then the map changed with bewildering rapidity. China, having lain unmoved for millennia, passed through all the stages from feudalism through capitalism to Communism in this century. History ran wild.

Mao was of rustic origins himself, and had fought his long civil war from grass roots. Defeated in the towns, he went on his Long March through the countryside, gathering support from the peasants. Thus, far from the bourgeois Kuomintang government encircling and repressing the Communists, it was ultimately they who encircled and repressed the Kuomintang. Having won his war, defeated the Nationalist forces, and established his government in Peking, Mao did not forget the peasants who made his triumph possible. This was a people's revolution, and the vast majority of the people worked in the fields. They were the priority.

As an army man, Mao was no stranger to starvation and knew the importance of grain. In fact he was obsessed by it. All else was secondary. The industrial revolution could wait, the agrarian one could not. If an army marched on its stomach, then so did a nation. China was on the move, and grain was its fuel. Not until the nation was agriculturally self-sufficient could it be secure and free from external control. Mao's great achievement was that he seized on the principles of Marx and Lenin and applied them to rural society. In a mere two years he transformed the country, collectivising agriculture, vesting all land in the state, and parcelling it out again to the people. He organised the peasants into communes, the communes into brigades, and the brigades into production teams. Mao was a military man. He saw things in military terms, and yet he regarded men as equals. How to reconcile the two was his problem. To make all men equal in their subservience to himself was his unhappy solution. Innocuous titles such as 'Chairman' and 'Helmsman' did little to disguise the absolute nature of his power.

Mao's massive irrigation projects of the fifties, bringing water to the fields in the traditional Chinese way, were something the people could understand and believe in. Here he mobilised and inspired the people to prodigious feats. They burrowed their way through mountains with spades and dammed their valleys with earth. He went some way to solving one of China's oldest problems – water – bringing it to places that needed it and stopping it from going to places that didn't.

Flooding and famine have dogged China throughout its history. The great rivers, Yangtse, Mekong and Huangho, are both lifeline and noose. They bring melted ice from the Himalayas to nourish the fields, and, in summer, flash floods to swamp them. Thousands died in 1981 when the Yangtse burst its banks. The Huangho or Yellow River, so called because of the colour of its waters, carries down more silt than any other; thirty times more than that other great irrigator of the ancient world, the Nile. After centuries of damming and deposition, its banks stand up like walls, fifteen feet high, from the plains of

Henan in the heart of China. When the Huangho bursts it
banks whole villages disappear. For this reason it is also know
as 'China's sorrow', yet in the very act of destruction it rejuv
enates the land. In hostile and mountainous terrain Mao'
irrigation schemes are a lasting achievement. His agricultura
plans are not. The 'Great Leap Forward' of the late fifties was a
flop. Based upon Western mechanisation and collective
Communism, Mao's plans for modernisation left the people
behind.

The people were organised into communes with massive
dining halls, schools and separate male and female dormitories
in order that they might work for the greater good of the state
and Chairman Mao. On the comfortable assumption that al
men would naturally work to the best of their ability, it wa
deemed unnecessary to see how much work they actually did. I
was enough to consider a person's age, strength, experience
sex, and 'political consciousness', and award him 'work points
accordingly. Like many Communist principles, this was mar
vellous in theory but it broke down in practice.

Famine stalked the land. Deng Xiao Ping saw the folly o
Mao's ways and, together with Liu Shaoqui, tried to remed
them. Liu replaced Mao as head of state, and urged a return
to the more traditional village way of life. Mao vehementl
attacked this as an invitation to bourgeois greed and avidity
and cast around for a means of ousting his opponents and
restoring himself to power. His agricultural revolution had
failed; perhaps a political revolution would succeed. An idealis
himself, who had watched men fight and die for their beliefs, he
was disillusioned with the apathy of the nation. He saw hi
failure as being due to bourgeois elements within society and
believed that the very people who had come to power with the
founding of the republic were now in turn entrenching them
selves as lofty bureaucrats. He himself of course was a tru
Communist, and exempt from such criticism. The fact that i
was his political opponents who would suffer in the politica
purge and himself who would be swept back to power wa
purely incidental. He exhorted the people to rise up against
the bourgeois elements amongst themselves. He ordered th
students to bombard the headquarters of government arme
with the slogan 'Out with the old, in with the new'. Bands c

youngsters roamed the countryside in groups – Red Brigades – extracting a brutal revenge on the bureaucracy.

All this was based on two of Mao's writings. First, a directive of 7 May 1966 amongst other things exhorted workers, students and officials to criticise the bourgeoisie, and work beside the peasants in the fields in order to become closer to the masses and to narrow 'the gap between workers and peasants, town and country, and mental and manual labour . . . in this way the whole country will become a great school of Mao Tse Tung thought'. Second, a speech of 4 October 1966 instructed the new cadres in the necessity of physical labour, saying that they too must work in the fields for fear of becoming comfortable bureaucrats. As recently as 1980, with education restored, school-leavers from the towns would be shipped off *en bloc* to work in the fields – some on a permanent basis. The dislocation, misery and bitterness which this caused is easy to imagine. The workers learned nothing from the peasants but the misery of their ways. The peasants learned nothing from the workers but that they were despised for their backwardness. The country was once more thrown into confusion. Mao attempted to salvage something of his doctrine by separating the peasants and workers once more and setting up special '7th May Schools' for the worker cadres, thus neatly negating the point of his plan. These, for the officials, were a lesson in nothing but their own ineptitude.

The nation lurched from catastrophe to catastrophe. The Red Brigades, freed from all restraint, ran wild, spreading chaos and confusion. The country was turned upside down. This 'Cultural Revolution' was a misnomer. It was Cultural Destruction, pure and simple. Nothing was put forward to replace what had gone before. Art, music, architecture and learning, all were trappings of the bourgeoisie and had to be rooted out and destroyed. All schools were closed, teachers and artists persecuted, priceless treasures smashed, temples and museums burnt, parents and grandparents mocked. Anything old was bad. All authority was tyrannical. The only true act was the revolutionary act and the revolutionary act was the act of destruction. The Red Brigades were buoyed up with the belief that they were ushering in a new era. No-one dared to face them; criticism was counter-revolutionary.

Even Mao saw the error of his ways by the end, but what could he do? He had tried everything and failed. The Cultural Revolution was not just a ploy to regain his personal power. He did genuinely believe in the Marxist cycle of revolution. Society had to keep revolving and cleansing itself until the advent of the perfect Communist society, when further revolution was impossible since everyone was in accord. But society did not like being stood on its head. It was a nightmare, and one which could only be brought to an end by the death of the dreamer – Mao. When this occurred in 1976, the nation breathed a communal sigh of relief, and the revolution was over.

Mao's old critic, Deng Xiao Ping, returned to power, bringing with him a down-to-earth brand of pragmatism. He introduced a new system of 'responsibility' to agriculture. This replaced Mao's 'work points'. Under the new system peasants are given tracts of land as their own responsibility, and a quota to fulfil in contract with their work brigade. Strip farming is back. They must produce their quota for the state, and anything above this they keep, store or sell as they please in the free markets springing up around the country. Here they can buy goods they want for cash, instead of swopping carefully regulated basic commodities for ration coupons. No one can tell them what to do or how to do it. Provided they fulfil their quota obligations they are free agents. These policies have been dramatically successful. There has been a rapid upsurge in production. The country harvests three times as much grain today as it did in the fifties, and is almost self-sufficient. For all Mao's rhetoric about the peasants, it is Deng Xiao Ping who has done most to improve their lot, considerably increasing the price of grain and thereby narrowing the gap between the earnings of peasants and workers. At the cost of a little inflation, Deng has transformed the state budget from a deficit of 5,000 million pounds in 1979 to a state of near balance today.

The people talk about the progressive reforms which Deng has introduced, but if one looks a little closer it becomes apparent that they are just a return to his plans of the sixties. With free markets and cottage industries re-emerging in the country, and bonuses and wage gradations in the factories, China and the West are not so far away from each other. As the East moves West and the West moves East, they may find common ground. China discovers the benefits of private industry and a market economy, while Europe finds the rewards of nationalisation and worker participation schemes. As Deng Xiao Ping says, 'What matter if the cat be black or white, so long as it catches mice.'

But has he gone too far? China's history is a pendulum swinging backwards and forwards, or, as Mao might have it, a wheel turning full circle. Already there are rumblings about the return of rural capitalism, the demise of collective communism, and the anarchy of agriculture. There are rumours that the ageing Deng is failing, and slipping into the 'second line' of politics. With recent purges in the administration taking place, perhaps the stage is ready for another change of scene.

As we approach Guilin (or Kweilin as it used to be spelt) we come upon the most incredible 'hillscape' I have ever seen. Sheer rock pinnacles rise out of the plain; vertical faces tower over the land; great stony fingers thrust up through the soil, each one separate and distinct; rock chimneys from some vast subterranean furnace; massive monoliths march away in serried ranks, the ossified guardians of another era. Bare crags lined with ledges support an old hardy tree, while shelving slopes, festooned with foliage, spill down the cliffs. The road threads between these silent sentinels, on level ground. Ahead, in a large clearing, lies Guilin, capital of Guangxi province.

In former times boats would come up river from Canton through Wuzhou to Guilin, and sail on north along the Ling canal all the way to the Yangtse basin. The canal is 2,200 years old, built by the first Qin Emperor to link the furthest flung parts of his realm to the centre. It was used to supply an army of half a million men who were conquering the Zhuang tribe to the south. The Zhuang are the largest minority group in China. They have always been an independent and warlike tribe and still dominate the lower half of the province. They were among the first to fight the Japanese in the Second World War and the last to accept the Communists thereafter. Guilin's population jumped from 100,000 to a million in the early forties as China fled the Japanese advance. An American fighting force, the Flying Tigers, were stationed here at that time. No matter what damage the Japanese bombers did to their runway overnight, it was always magically restored by thousands of Chinese hands before morning.

Today the province is known as the Guangxi Zhuang Autonomous Region and is one of the five semi-autonomous areas surrounding central China, the other four being Tibet to the west, and Xinjiang, Ningxiu and Inner Mongolia to the north. These form a buffer zone between Han China and the outside world.

We find a hotel and go for a walk through town. Guilin means 'Cassia forest', and the streets are lined with osmanthus and cinnamon trees (Chinese cassia.) Sadly, much of the town has recently been rebuilt as a result of Japanese bombing in the Second World War, but the beauty of the surrounding area remains. On return we find a Chinaman waiting outside the gates who eagerly introduces himself as Don. It soon becomes apparent that Don is interested in more than just practising his English. Guilin is the most popular tourist spot in southern China for visitors from Hong Kong and elsewhere. As a result, it is reputedly the only place in China where you can change money on the black market.

Tourists swop their special exchange certificates for local remninbi-yuan. Most people get about thirteen units of local currency for ten units of tourist money. During my stay, however, I read a newspaper report stating that tourist money was changing hands for two or three times its face value in Xian. This did not surprise me. A certain amount of corruption is inherent in Chinese bureaucracy. Quite why tourist money is in such demand is something of a mystery to me. In other parts of the world people amass foreign currency to enable them to leave the country. But tourist money is not foreign money and it is not exchangeable abroad. The explanation must lie in the Friendship Stores. In these special shops, which exist only in major towns, politicians and foreigners can buy luxury goods unavailable elsewhere. Friendship Stores only accept tourist money. Perhaps Chinamen are willing to accept this unbalanced rate of exchange for the sake of those goods.

Don the Chinaman changes money with us, and takes a little extra in order to buy us tickets for a boat trip down the River Xianjlang or Li, a branch of the Pearl which runs past Canton. He is insistent that our dealing should take place in his friend's restaurant. This is a tourist restaurant with white cloths on the tables, catering for wealthy visitors from Hong Kong. The food is expensive and cooked out of sight in a separate kitchen. I am suspicious and would rather go to one of the crowded cheap restaurants down the road, favoured by the local people. Don is not keen on this. Not surprisingly we find that he himself is not hungry, but he assures us that this is the only place for Westerners to eat and that we should not risk eating in a local restaurant. I am not convinced. I would rather trust the habits of local Chinamen who have lived here all their lives, than foreign visitors who come for a day. It seems, however, that this is all part of the package deal which Don is providing.

This reminds me of accounts of early traders dealing with China in the nineteenth century. The Chinese are extremely canny businessmen, as I'm sure the West will again discover in the course of building up its trading links. Early merchants paint a picture of subtle negotiating taking place in civilised surroundings – neither of which our somewhat piratical pioneers were accustomed to. All the formalities must be abided by. They form an integral part of the transaction, and who is to know where the real significance of the bargain lies? Even if money is the primary consideration you can be sure that it is not the straightforward transaction it seems to be.

In our case we changed money at what seemed a reasonable rate of exchange, without any idea of the real value of the notes we were handing over. We ate an expensive meal for which I'm sure our friend got a healthy commission. We gave him money so that he could buy us tickets for the boat trip, but we paid in tourist vouchers. It was to prove the same all over China. It was impossible to pay people for services, for that would reduce them to the status of servants. A more subtle solution had to be found to make the transaction look like an exchange of favours. A Chinaman buys your train ticket for you if you pay him the fare in tourist vouchers. He can then make his profit by exchanging them, and everyone will be happy, but to attempt to pay in remninbi and give him a little extra for his trouble would be insulting.

The unfortunate result of all this wheeling and dealing is a severe stomach ache for me next morning. For all the expense of the meal, I think that we were served up a piece of rotten old dog which is a speciality here. Had I been left to my own devices this would never have happened. I feel resentful. Perhaps that's just a part of being ill.

The next day I am sufficiently recovered for our boat trip. Very early in the morning, before dawn, we cause much consternation by boarding the ordinary Chinese bus to go to the river. Thanks to Don we find two seats reserved for us on the bus. Eventually we manage to persuade the worried driver to start his engine, and off we go, along the one broad road leading out of town, past the flats being built on the outskirts, and into the fields. The rock sentinels rise up on either side from the morning mist: we plunge down a side road, between two of them, to the river.

Three large steamers are moored beside a little village. Shops on the bank sell handkerchiefs, cloisonné, embroidery and watercolours. The ships hoot. We walk up the gang-plank and cast off, but before we have moved far from the bank, a truck comes roaring down the hill, horn blaring. A group of soldiers in their green great-coats jump down and come rushing along the jetty, gesticulating madly. Everyone laughs. The captain turns the wheel and the bows nudge back into the bank just long enough for them to jump aboard.

We sit, rather ridiculously, on wooden chairs set out in rows on the enclosed deck. A gangway and rail run around the outside, but it is much too cold to stand out there. The keel of the boat scrapes against gravel and stones as we move into mid-stream. You can see the bottom just a few feet away. In spring boats come right the way upstream of Guilin from the coast, but at this time of year they stop at Wuzhou. Only the sampans and these flat-bottomed barges can navigate the upper reaches of the Li.

The cliffs rise up sheer from the water; their jagged edges loom together far above like giant pincers, or the clashing jaws of the legendary Simplaides. On a fine day their image is reflected perfectly in the water. If you stare long enough, nyads will steal away your senses till you know not which is the mountain and which the watery illusion.

Curious caves and tunnels have been carved by wind and water along faults in the rock. Each one has its story. The Chinese are an imaginative people and see all sorts of animals and characters trapped in the shape of rocks. Some of these stretch the Western mind a little far, though I certainly see my fair share of elephants, camels, unicorns, and white horses. However the chill of the wind, the gloom of the sky and the state of my stomach prevent me from appreciating them to the full.

I am somewhat relieved when we reach the village of Yang-shuo with its charming cliff path along the waterfront. There is an old Chinese saying: 'The scenery of Guilin is the best under heaven, but that of Yangshuo is even better.' A coach is waiting to take us back to Guilin and me to bed.

Our friend Don, with a finger in every pie, provides us with two bicycles for the day. This is the only way to see the far-flung sites around Guilin.

Beneath a clear sky we pedal down to the river at Elephant Rock. This is a hump-backed peninsula wading out into the water, with a large hole pierced through it near the end. The rock pillar left on the far side looks like an elephant's trunk dipping down into the river.

We get an old lady to ferry us across in her punt to the Elephant, and sit on a rock ledge at the bottom of the cavern watching the fishermen at work on the river. Their boats, or perhaps floats would be a better word, consist of four bamboo trunks strapped together and curling slightly up at either end. Here they stand or squat a few inches above the water, line in hand, patiently awaiting the fish. Next to them, and in the same hunched posture, perch cormorants. They too are out fishing. Carefully trained from fledglings, they will suddenly swoop into the water, pluck out a startled fish in their long beaks and take it back to their master. In the course of a long day it is not unknown for master and bird to take a break and share a raw fish together. While we watch, neither man nor bird catches anything or even moves. The river swims in spreading menisci to the horizon; floating fishermen etched into its glassy surface seem poised for effect rather than purpose, painted on to the perspective by some master artist. This mirror holds, as it were, the mirror up to nature, and reflecting there, makes it doubly beautiful.

We move across the river to Pagoda Hill, a limestone finger rising out of the plain, splintered off from the surrounding hills and encircled with a winding staircase around its buttresses. From the top we gain marvellous views of the area. The fertile flats of the Li, covered in varying hues of vegetable green, stretch out to the massing hills. Nearby, dusty old farm buildings with brightly tiled interlocking roofs lie behind mud walls, hidden from all but the birds and those atop Pagoda Hill. Further west, the fields take on wider dimensions, and the large blunt buildings of a commune rise up in the shadow of the hills.

The sun beats down as we descend the baking staircase and climb on to our bicycles. A picture of a drink on a sign outside a house draws us into the shade at the side of the road. We go up the stairs to find the door boarded shut and dust an inch thick on the floor.

Soon the tall gates of a commune loom up on our left. We ride between them and come upon people, very orderly people all dressed in blue Mao suits, walking along carefully laid out concrete paths, or queuing, bowl in hand, outside the massive dining hall. Long low buildings which look like factories but could be dormitories line the path. An enormous square sports ground is cut into the hillside. A saying of Chairman Mao is inscribed in huge characters on the retaining walls. Troops of workers in long lines are doing exercises to a female voice booming out through loudspeakers.

These old-fashioned speakers are a prominent feature of commune life. Even in the fields round about, you can find them strapped to old trees or posts. This is the only way the Party can convey its propaganda to the masses living in the country. Blanket indoctrination through constant repetition was Mao's way of building up the political consciousness of the people. The thoughts of Chairman Mao were beamed daily across the country, snaking their way through a million cables to loud speakers in the fields. Workers in the factories and communes had to get used to this constant background noise. What did they think of it, I wonder?

These massive propaganda campaigns largely came to an end at the death of Mao. They achieved the opposite of their purpose, disrupting rather than uniting the country. Many of the speakers have gone. Those that remain, likely as not, will be playing classical music now, both Chinese and Western, and even the Russian composers are represented today, by Tchaikovsky and Rimsky-Korsakov.

Previously a Westerner would have been welcomed and shown round a commune, but now the Chinese are not so proud of their system, and no one seems inclined to speak to us. Not wishing to intrude, we circle round and out through the gates again.

John turns left and goes up into the hills, I turn right towards the park. At the entrance of the park I am surprised to meet my friend Don.

'What are you doing here?' I ask.

'I am a guide here,' he replies.

'But you should be working in the factory making valves for radios.'

'Oh, that is just a few hours each day.'

'Why is that?'

'There is not enough work for everyone, so we share it around. That way, everyone is able to contribute. In the morning we have communal exercises, and twice a week discuss political theory, but in the afternoons I am a guide.'

This all comes out rather pat as if it is part of his guided tour. Underneath, however, I get the impression that Don thinks it all nonsense. I also guess that his position as guide is something of a self-appointment. His English is excellent. He's a bright boy but he's playing a dangerous game. He's cornered a tourist market, and, in Chinese terms, is earning a fortune, but the next time the authorities clamp down, he could be the first to go. Already the net is closing in and he is no longer welcome around the hotel.

'Please bring the bicycles back to me by the bridge at 6 p.m.,' he says, 'and bring along the two Scandinavians who arrived at your hotel today. Say that Paul wants to see them.'

Surprised that Don brooks any rival, but amused to find myself caught up in his tangled scheme of things, I agree, and watch him arrow off in pursuit of another pale face on the horizon.

I tour round the park and head back to the hotel at 5.45. I find two Scandinavians by the entrance. 'Are you waiting for Paul?' I ask. They nod. 'Follow me.' I pick up the other bicycles and lead on.

It's getting dark. As we approach the bridge, Don steps out of the shadows and comes to meet us. One of the Swedes puts out his hand and Don grasps it (though the gesture doesn't come quite naturally to him yet).

'Hello, Paul,' he says.

'Hello,' replies Don.

'I thought you were called Don,' I observe to Don.

'A man can have many names,' he replies rather enigmatically. He turns back to the Swede. 'Here are your bicycles for tomorrow. Shall we go and eat?'

Not me, not this time. I almost warn the Swedes, but hold back from some misplaced feeling of loyalty to Don. We are accomplices in crime, united by that peculiar bond which joins the underworld fraternity.

'I'll leave you to it,' I say. 'I'm going to the theatre.'

I turn on my heel and escape into the darkness. The warm glow of a restaurant further up the road lures me in to stare at the hieroglyphic menu hanging on the whitewashed wall. I look at it for a minute to find out what money to have ready, totally ignorant as usual of what I might be paying for.

'You read Chinese?' comes a voice from behind. I turn round and am amazed to see a toothless old man staring at me.

'No. Do you speak English?'

'My English is very poor, but I help you what to eat. Sweet and sour pork is very good.'

'All right. Here is some money. Please can you get some sweet and sour pork for both of us?'

'No, no, I not hungry; I get for you.'

He weaves off on bandy legs to order the meal, protesting the while his absence of hunger. He is different from the others: an individual, set apart not only by his ability to speak English, but also by his clothes. He wears coarse trousers of sack-cloth, with a thick fustian jacket. They are the clothes of a rustic, brown instead of blue. He is too old and set in his ways to worry about the latest Party directive.

He returns with my pork in a thick red sauce. The room, formerly white and angular, now seems warm and friendly as he sits across the round table from me. It's difficult to hold a conversation while eating, for the Chinese are not too fussy about cutting meat off the bone when preparing food. Chop

chop, chop with a great metal cleaver on a wooden board, and in it all goes into the cauldron. They leave you to struggle with mouthfuls of bone and extract what goodness you can from it. Perhaps this is another example of the thrift, rather than the laziness, of the Chinese people. A lot of goodness can be derived from sucking old bones, and the Chinese seem to gain much pleasure from doing so, but I have a certain difficulty. I have just about mastered the art of transporting food with chopsticks from my plate to my mouth, without spreading too much of it over the floor, the return journey from mouth to plate is an entirely different matter. Bits of chewed bone seem determined to throw themselves everywhere. How, I wonder, would the toothless old man opposite me manage such a meal? What an enigma he is. Smiling and sitting on the far side of the table: patiently waiting and watching. There is something strange about his speech. Not so much the sounds he makes, which are amazingly accurate, but the words he chooses. I have to ask him.

'Where did you learn to speak English?'

'Christian missionaries taught me to speak English. I learnt from the Bible long time ago.'

He must be well over seventy.

'You know that it will be Christmas soon?' I ask.

'Yes, but we do not have Christmas in China. There are no more churches. All gone.'

'And the missionaries? They are gone too?'

'All gone. Long time ago. Sorry, we have no Christmas.'

'Are you Christian?'

'Yes. We two Christian.'

He watches with polite interest as I wrestle with the last of my pork.

'Thank you for speaking with me,' he says, 'May you be happy in China.'

I shake his hand and go out of the door: 'Goodbye.' There's so much I want to ask the old man but I don't want to get him into trouble. I hurry through the cold night wondering whether he is really Christian or only saying that to please me.

Here of all places in China it is possible. Jesuit missionaries gained a toehold in China at the end of the sixteenth century, though it was their gift of a mechanical clock and ability to cast cannon that initially impressed the Emperor, the 'Son of Heaven', rather than their religious beliefs. They were given permission to found a church in Peking in 1602 and were gradually accepted at court. When the Manchus captured Peking in 1644, the Jesuits fled south to Guilin with the Ming court and finally converted the Royal Household to Christianity. Christianity made progress in the south throughout the eighteenth and nineteenth centuries, but was finally discredited in the Taiping Rebellion. In 1851 Hung Hsui Chuan, a village school teacher who had failed the Imperial examinations four times, by chance read some Christian pamphlets, which led him to the happy realisation that he was the younger son of Jesus Christ. Armed with this belief, he roused the masses of the peasants in a holy war against the Manchus to establish the Heavenly Kingdom of Peace, or Taiping Tienko. By 1853 he had captured Nanjing and held most of the south under his control. He then looked east to Shanghai and his European 'allies' who had brought Christianity to the land and would surely support the holy cause. But the British were already quite happy dealing with the weak Manchu Emperor and saw the creation of a Heavenly Kingdom as a threat to their own position. They therefore sent a force against the Taipings under the command of Gordon (who later came to fame in Khartoum), which broke the rebellion. The Heavenly Kingdom of Peace was at an end. It had cost 20 million lives. If Europeans were capable of such treachery, neither Europeans nor Christianity were to be tolerated. The West had lost its chance to convert China to Christianity. Britain had sown the seeds of xenophobic discontent which came to fruition nearly half a century later in the Boxer rebellion when the people rose up to eject the foreign devils from the land.

While my thoughts thus wander, my feet have followed the bend of the river round to the town theatre. Going to the theatre in China is a unique experience. With no great tradition of instrumental music, and the transistorised onslaught of television and stereo yet to come, the theatre stands alone as the focus of popular entertainment. It is a great family occasion. Granddaughters sit on their grandfathers' knees, while workers turn round in their seats to chat to friends behind them. The audience is not slow to join in with cheers and clapping where merited. Plays, ballets, acrobatics and above all, opera, are all enjoyed in the same way. The level of success of a Chinese show can be gauged by the level of noise of its audience, general hubbub rather than quiet concentration being the sign of popular acclaim. But it has not always been thus.

When Chiang Ching, Mao's wife (herself an actress from Shanghai), banned Peking opera during the Cultural Revolution and reduced the number of permissible Chinese operas from 1,300 to eight, she earned herself the hatred of a nation. First she used her power to destroy anyone who she imagined had slighted her in the past, then she used her own grotesque sensibilities to produce eight revolutionary model operas and a handful of model ballets. She believed that there is no art for art's sake. Art must be revolutionary and representational. Non-representational classical music is decadent and not to be endured. Subtlety is to be avoided and crude repetition encouraged. The people must not mistake the message. Theatre should be used to develop the political awareness of the people.

Attendance, not surprisingly, was not a joy but an obligation. Tickets could not be bought. They were issued in strict rotation. Anyone failing to attend risked criticism as showing counter-revolutionary tendencies. Some idea of the cultural dearth that resulted can be gained from a look at the titles of permitted operas such as *The Taking of Tiger Mountain by Storm*, *The Red Brigade of Women*, or the songs: 'The light that shines from Chairman Mao', 'I have seen Chairman Mao', 'The night soil collectors are coming down the Mountain'. All the while, in private, Chiang Ching was showing her favourite Greta Garbo films to selected friends. By 1981, however, the awareness of the people was such that they realised what she had been doing and consigned her to prison, together with the rest of the 'gang of four'.

Not surprisingly, since her imprisonment there has been a resurgence in music and theatre in China. Western music is once again popular. The Boston Symphony Orchestra played to packed audiences on its recent tour of China. Even the progressive sound of Jean-Michel Jarre was welcomed by the People's Republic, though some confusion arose before his first performance when they discovered he needed electricity to play his music. Electricity and music are not things naturally linked in the Chinese mind.

Pictures are still hard to come by. The little art I can find is over-priced and aimed at the tourist. You would not expect to see a picture on a Chinese wall. Luxury possessions are left to the bourgeoisie. There are, however, some pictures displayed on the walls of the theatre foyer. I look at these until a loud bell sends me rushing, on a wave of excitement in a sea of blue, to the darkened pit of the stalls. The curtain rises, accompanied by a sigh of anticipation from the audience, to reveal a tree, firmly planted in the middle of the stage, as big and solid as any you could find in any lowland forest. A valley dwindles back into the perspective. A man leaps out from behind the tree. The show has begun. The Tibetan dance troop unfolds its plot with an athletic fluidity I have never seen before. Scenery and effects are superb. Chinese ingenuity combines with a little Western technical know-how to weave a magical tale from Tibetan folk legend. Astral images float over translucent screens, flashing lights beneath billowing smoke, brilliant costumes before painted backdrops. Figures whirl about the stage until the final curtain falls, sending the people bubbling back once more to their homes.

5

Dragon's Bones in Kunming

 I FEEL strange again as I wake up today. The sweet and sour pork last night was not, I think, a good idea. I have to get up, however, to buy some warm clothes for the mountains. 7 a.m. The day is already old for most Chinese. I visit one of the big grey department stores. This one actually has blue walls, but somehow I always think of these stores as grey. Perhaps it is the over-cast morning or the dismal choice that lends the place this gloomy aspect. Piles of clothes stack up on shelves to the ceiling, all blue, all the same price, their only distinguishing feature being the labels telling you their measurements. Thick wollen under-garments like track suits line the shelves. The Chinese are very susceptible to cold, and delight in piling on layer upon layer of clothing, four or five thick, till they can hardly move. I have seen children so padded that they have to hold their arms out at right angles above their jackets; they are so round that you feel that they would bounce if they fell over. Here at least the Chinese allow themselves a little colour, lavishing all their care and money on dressing baby. Granny sits up knitting him bright hat and mittens, while Mummy might conjure up a patterned coat. Chairman Mao obviously never designed any suits for the under-fives. The only thing that stops the Chinese toddler from winning best-dressed baby awards is the rather undignified rent in the back of his trousers. While the rest of him is protected in an impene-trable layer of clothing, his nether regions are exposed to the vagaries of the Chinese weather. Practical, no doubt, but scarcely

61

comfortable. I felt rather sorry for the owner of the first such bare
behind I saw waddling along the pavement. 'Fancy his mother
doing that to him,' I thought, but as I saw thousands of his
peers thus similarly exposed, I was forced to shrug my shoulders and put it down as just another of those Oriental mysteries.

In the corner of the shop are the enormous green greatcoats
that Chinese soldiers wear. I try one on. Lined with great
swathes of cotton it is stiflingly hot, heavy and unwieldy. It
could double as armour-plating or a tent in an emergency. I'm
sure if I crept out of it, it would continue to stand up like a little
pyramid in the corner of the shop. It is not practical for my
purposes. If I bought it, I would have to wear it all the time. Not
many people wear these coats outside the militia. It is the
lifestyle of the people, rather than the cost of the article, that
accounts for this. In a land without central heating, where the
temperature of the houses and the streets in the towns is the
same, coats become irrelevant. In the country, where people
have fires to keep their houses warm, they are largely irrelevant
too. At first light the men get up and go to work in the field. At
dusk they come home, eat and go to bed. As yet there is no place
for the luxury of coats in China.

In another corner of the shop are the scarves. To my
surprise I find, as well as knotted blue scarves, some wonderfully soft brown and grey ones, more expensive, and closely
woven from cashmere wool. I buy one of these and a pair of
gloves, but can't seem to find a hat to suit me. The Chinese are
very keen on hats. Once again, considering the amount of body
heat lost through the head, this is not so much an idle decoration as a necessity in winter. All I can find are little green or blue
peaked caps, or great wool-lined hats with huge flaps coming
down to cover the ears. What I want is something in between.

I pay for my scarf, wrap it round my neck, and step outside.
On the corner of the street a ring of squatting men share a small
circle of warmth as nuts bake over a charcoal fire. Off to the
right the road seems unusually crowded. On closer inspection I
find my first street-market. There's a greater variety of clothes
here. In the midst of it is a man selling a curious sort of grey felt
hat. They are stacked up on his table, one inside the other, like
grey casseroles. They have enormous turn-ups all round the
sides. He picks one up to demonstrate its use. For normal wear

it sits on your head like a pudding bowl, but when a gale or snowstorm blows up, you unroll the turn-up till it comes down your neck, leaving a small slit for your eyes like a medieval visor. I get one of these devices for its novelty value if nothing else. Thus suitably equipped, I return to the hotel to kick John out of bed (no mean task), and off we go to the natural wonders of the 'reed flute' caves.

We pursue a guide through twisting tunnels, following faults in the limestone rock, into underground caverns and secret chambers deep under the hill. Strange to think of all this space within this rock. No one would have guessed it from the outside. Over the centuries tiny particles of limestone in solution have dripped down to form groves of bamboo, organ pipes, spears and fluted columns on the floor, while candelabra and jellyfish hang down from the ceiling. At the end of a vast cave you can see the London skyline in silhouette. It doesn't take much imagination to pick out the dome of St Paul's and the Post Office tower.

I am thankful to reach the end of the tour. My stomach is bad. John goes on to the park while I head back to the hotel. I have that peculiar detached feeling that one gets with fever. As I walk through the streets I am not really there. I could do anything I want and no one would notice. The world passes by as in a vision. Everything is moving except me. I'm looking at the world through the window of a train. I smile at people graciously for a moment, before they are whisked away into the past, never to be seen again.

The gates of my hotel loom into view. I watch my feet mount the steps, like a television camera in a Hitchcock thriller. The bed comes towards me, and suddenly I'm floating face down upon it. I mustn't move; I don't want to sink. Must stay still. Stop moving.

A moment later something shakes my arm, I swim up from a great depth and break the surface in my hotel room beneath harsh yellow lights. John is shaking me.

'Wake up, it's time to go.'

'Go where? What time is it?'

'It's seven in the evening, and time to catch the overnight train to Kunming.'

'I don't feel very well.'

'But it's Christmas Eve.'

'That doesn't make me feel any better.'

'Don's got us tickets with the two Swedes for the 8 p.m. train. As soon as we get on board, we'll find you a sleeper and you can lie down again.'

I'm really not well enough to travel, but John wants to go. I might as well be making progress lying in bed in a train as stationary in a hotel.

'O.K., let's go.'

I haul myself up, pack my rucksack and join the two Swedes. The short walk to the station assumes a peculiar intensity. I feel the air flow in and out of my lungs like an ebb-tide. The world takes on the larger-than-life quality of a Van Gogh painting. Shapes and images vie with one another for my attention. A lamp hanging from a low beam in a wooden shop bathes an old woman in an ethereal halo: bright saucers round a shroud. Why does she stand so still beneath that shawl? What is she hiding there – a skull? The lantern in the next shop, set in motion by an unseen force, swings to and fro, sending shafts of light coruscating off rows of green bottles on the shelves.

'Wait a moment,' says John, getting out some money. He hands over a note. The woman squints at it, then pockets it happily: tourist money. John picks four large bottles and catches us up. 'Well, it is Christmas Eve,' he explains.

We turn a corner and see the station: large, squat, and planted on six steps. I go up these into the huge waiting hall and lie down on a bench. Think of one thing at a time. Don't try to do too much. Eight o'clock comes and goes. Strange. Chinese trains are supposed to run on time. John goes to find out what has happened and comes back with an official.

'Come on,' he says, 'He's taking us to the first class waiting room. The train has been delayed.'

Down more steps, clinking of keys, and in we go to a cold dark waiting room. The official smiles, turns a switch, and a bare bulb throws the room into relief. Large armchairs line the walls. Newspapers in various languages, one of them English, lie on a table by the door. It seems even colder than the hall. There, at least, was a certain warmth between the fellow waiting passengers. Here I feel isolated, cut off and forgotten. Why do they always try to segregate us? The official seems apologetic.

We should never have gone to the big hall. He doesn't know that Don the Chinaman bought us our ticket. I wish I could lie down in the big hall again. Sitting in a chair is not good for me. I change my position every few minutes. This is the only activity that marks the passage of time in the waiting room. Not even a pendulum rocks. The others read. The hours go by. Have they forgotten us? Has the train gone? John finds the official again but cannot make him understand.

'Show him the ticket, John.'

'Kunming, yes, Kunming.'

I think the message has got through. He knows where we want to go. The people are still there in the big hall. The train has not arrived yet. I still feel ill. Nothing has changed. Perhaps the train will never come. No, here is the official with his keys again. Got to move again. The train is here.

'Come on. We'll head for the hard sleepers. Friend Don says they always keep a few spares for VIPs.'

But Don is not always right, and there are no hard beds left – or we are not VIPs, I'm not sure which. Could this be a final cynical joke he has played on the decadent Westerners, I wonder.

All the while we are trying to get hard beds, the hard seats are filling up. By the time we arrive, we have to fight for standing room. The coachman doesn't want us there: 'Soft bed, soft bed, why don't you take soft bed?'

'Why don't you give me hard bed?'

'No hard bed. You soft bed, soft bed.'

My hard seat (or in this case, hard stand) costs me £3. A soft bed is £30. They won't get me in there till I'm dead – perhaps later on tomorrow morning. Sitting on the floor is out of the question, due to the Chinese habit of exorcising the throat demon. The Chinese spit everywhere, all the time. They break off conversations, make the most appalling gurgling noises in their throats, spit all over the floor and continue as if nothing has happened. I think they regard it rather like coughing, and do it almost as instinctively. They spit on the streets, on the sidewalks, on the trains, on the buses, in the shops, in the restaurants, in the fields, in the towns, everywhere. In winter they all spit and they all have colds but they don't connect the two. They believe it is healthy to spit: it gets rid of the evil fluids.

While there is an element of truth in this, what they don't realise is that it spreads them around. I am told that a national anti-spitting campaign has been launched. I have seen this elsewhere in Asia. In Hong Kong, for example, you can see posters saying: 'Spitting is filthy. Only animals spit.'

I can't honestly say that I've seen many animals spitting, but the sentiment is right. While I've no idea what any of the posters in China say, if any of them refer to spitting, they have made precious little impact on the population. But we should not judge others too quickly. My grandfather used to live in West Africa. When the natives first saw him using a handkerchief, they thought it was disgusting: 'Whenever he blows his nose,' they would say, 'he keeps it and puts it back in his pocket.' Indians, when they first saw the British taking baths, used to wonder at the sahibs wallowing like pigs in their own dirt.

One thing some Chinese do now is wear gauze masks over their nose and mouth. Quite whether these are used by people who have already got colds and want to avoid spreading them around, or people without colds who want to remain thus, I'm not sure. Either way, it seems a good idea, and is the nearest I've seen them get to pocket handkerchiefs. Whatever the cultural justifications for spitting, one thing is certain, it doesn't improve train floors.

We stand in silence. My fever makes me thirsty, but they have run out of boiled water on the train. What a nightmare. I look at my watch: 1 a.m. – Christmas Day. I can't work up the enthusiasm to tell the others; I would feel stupid saying 'Happy Christmas' in the circumstances, and to think that I'd been looking forward to my ride on a Chinese train! I'd heard so much about their cleanness and efficiency.

At 4 a.m. a hard sleeper becomes free. The others kindly let me have it. A mere instant later, or so it seems, my watch alarm wakes me with a painful whine: 7.30 a.m. I force myself out of my bunk and give it to John. Making my way along to the dining car for a little tea or soup, I find it closed. Where was I at 6 a.m. when all self-respecting Chinese got up? I try to go back, to sit in the relative comfort of the hard sleepers, but find that I've been locked out. A tiny dictator, armed with a set of keys, guards the door of each carriage. Without a ticket, you shall not ass. Don't they know that foreign guests must be treated with espect? It's strange. After days of privileged treatment one egins to regard it as one's due.

At 6 p.m. another bunk is free, and I collapse into it. At 7 p.m. ohn shakes me awake. Time for our Christmas dinner with the wedes. It's the last thing I want, but I feel I ought to make the ffort. It is Christmas after all. I try a little food. It immediately nakes me ill again, and I have to leave. On my way out, a ickening little Shanghai official grabs me, afraid, I suppose, hat I'm trying to sneak off without paying. I end up paying for veryone, and I didn't eat anything myself. Where's my sense of Christian charity gone this Christmas?

At 6 a.m. the next morning I am woken by scores of Chinese rying to sit on my bunk. Luckily we arrive at Kunming two ours later, before my temper can deteriorate any further. An nterminable ride in a taxi brings us to the hotel where, after nuch bargaining, we secure two rooms. Now, one last thing efore I let myself collapse. I must see a doctor. Yes, a doctor. inally I make the hotel clerk, who speaks a little English, nderstand, and I get the normal vaguely pointing finger in esponse: 'No, you come with me,' I say. I need a guide and an nterpreter. As always in these hotels the desk is grossly over-nanned, and the two others can hold the fort while he's away. Eventually I persuade him. He comes scurrying round from ehind his desk at great speed, and, with me in tow, leads on to he doctor who works at the back of the hotel. I recount my ymptoms through the clerk, and am given three different pills o be taken four times a day. Somewhat startled by his own isplay of initiative, and frightened lest someone find him away rom his post, the clerk leaves me to pay and hurries back to the otel. Safely installed in his little bureaucratic chink in the hotel oyer, he is able to summon up a smile as I come in through the oor again. Up to my room. Now I can collapse into bed.

I feel as if there's a tiny lizard trying to gnaw its way out of my tomach. I hope these pills cure it. When other people don't do vhat I tell them that's one thing, but when my own body refuses o do what it's told, that's quite another. I refused to be ill in Guilin, and as a result I am ill in Kunming.

Three days later the gnawing pain abates, and I begin to take a little interest in my surroundings. If I had to fall ill anywhere,

it might as well be here. This is the best hotel I've been in. Rug
line the floor of my room; heavy curtains drape across a fin
view of town; there's a writing desk in the corner, two soft bec
with bedside lights, a constant supply of hot water in thermo
flasks, and, despite our written note presented on arrival,
bathroom. Hot tea in a hot bath proves wonderfully medicina
and I feel well enough to try a few vegetables in the restaurar
downstairs. The body can teach you many things if you onl
know how to listen to it. The thought of meat appals me at th
moment but I have a craving for vegetables. The doctor told m
to avoid pork and eat vegetables.

Traditional Chinese doctors know how to listen to a body
and they don't use a stethoscope. They can learn all they nee
to know just by taking your pulse – though they may spen
hours doing so. Chinese medicine cannot claim the West'
dramatic successes in eliminating such killers as polio, smal
pox, malaria and measles, but it can be astonishingly effectiv
in its own way. Mashed toad, lizard's gizzards, dragon bon
crushed coal and assorted fungi may not sound exactly pala
able, but they do seem to work, and can frighten off a commo
cold, which is more than all our drugs and antibiotics can do. I
you are ill, you go to a doctor and describe your symptoms. H
will get down a different jar of pills or powders for each of you
complaints. This may result in your taking up to forty pills
day, but you will get better in the end. Ironically, at a time whe
Western medicine is making great inroads to the Orient, an
'bare foot doctors' are spreading the rules of rudimentar
hygiene to the most isolated of villages, traditional herb;
remedies are becoming increasingly popular in the West.

Scientists are taking Chinese methods seriously. A team (
American doctors came to study acupuncture and stayed in th
hotel last week. This peculiarly Chinese discipline has ha
spectacular success both as curative and anaesthetic. Typicall
Chinese, it is cheap and simple (when you know how) has n
side effects, and can actually enable a patient to participate i
his own operation. Although half a million Chinese a year ar
willing to undergo operations with nothing but a few needle
stuck into them to ease the pain, this treatment has yet to b
accepted in the West. It is not just a matter of persuading th
doctors, but the patients also. Faith, both in illness and in healtl

has a powerful effect. One thing is certain, I feel better today, and if it's taken dragon bones to cure me then I believe in dragons.

The two Swedes leave today and a French-Canadian, Jean-Pierre, arrives at the hotel. He's a student from Quebec on a holiday of indefinite length from the university. He's from India, where he's spent the last six months and his favourite expression is 'holy cow, man'. Maybe he tended the sacred cows out there. Jean-Pierre has heard that the Kunming Public Security Bureau gives visas to visit Simao and Jinghong to the south, by the Burma border. We tried to get these in Canton and were refused, but in China it is always worth another go. One day a man will tell you the rules state this, or that this is the price, and you won't be able to shift him. The next day a different man will give you a completely different story. I don't feel well enough for a whole day out, so I take Jean-Pierre's, John's and my own passport to the visa office and look around town while they are being processed.

Kunming has always been on the furthest border of the Empire. Sometimes it was one side of it, sometimes the other. It took the fighting strength of Kublai Khan in the thirteenth century finally to establish it within the boundaries of the realm. It was as a result of another invader this century that it rose to prominence. In the 1940s the refugees from the Japanese advance in the East swelled its numbers which now stand at 2 million. It is the capital of Yunnan province, which means 'South of the Clouds'. Kunming, 'Eternal Spring', is situated on the edge of the Himalayas. The air has a crystal quality to it, a purity that is rarely found in the post-industrial-revolution towns of the West. Wonderfully gnarled trees line the streets casting shadowed skeins over the pavement like the fractured glaze of an old Ming vase. The streets converge on the great concrete square that stands at the centre of every Chinese town. Huge and symmetrical, it is a man-made field to remind the people who crawl over its surface how insignificant is the individual compared to the might of the state. It is so big there is a tram stop at each corner to help you cross the void.

The old part of town lying on the banks of the canal is alive with activity; a startling contrast to the eerie space of the square. Here is an open air market. Old men stand round a

barrel full of meat, each holding a wooden stick and diligently
poking the dull but gleaming flesh, searching for just the right
cut. Next to this is a pile of curious saucer-like objects. Every so
often someone picks one up, weighs it, and pays for it, but I
cannot conceive what they might be. I move closer and am
amazed to discover stacks of pigs' heads, boned, and squashed
flat as pancakes, the tips of their noses now lying on the same
latitude as the ends of their ears. It's as if a herd of pigs has been
taken up in an aeroplane and dropped head-first from a great
height on to the concrete of the great square.

Further on in a corner shop men dip long thin doughnut
sticks into a white liquid in large bowls. Milk! I haven't seen or
tasted milk since coming to China. Dairy products are not a
normal feature of the Chinese market. Apparently the people do
not like them, besides which, any land which can support
anything is under rice (or wheat in the north). There is no grass
left for grazing. In my time in China I haven't seen a single cow.
Milk and meat, save for pork from the pigs that snuffle round
in the dirt, are things the majority of the population do without. Having downed two steaming bowls of this nectar, and
even consumed a little frozen as ice-cream, I continue on my
way.

Two-storeyed houses stretch away in unbroken lines.
Undulating eaves fretted with carvings are covered with the
faded colours of former days. An occasional gate ajar affords a
glimpse into an age gone by: a courtyard, surrounded on the
second floor by a wooden balcony, sacks of corn lying against
the wall, a stone well with wrought-iron stanchions. The
ghostly rustle of silk and flutter of fans seem to flit round about
on the edge of consciousness.

A shop sells polished stone, beloved of the Chinese. Rainbow
marble prised from the earth, hacked from the hills with axe
and adze, polished to a burning lustre of which it never
dreamed in its dark lonely days within the rock, then buried
once more in a velvet casket. Dense, cool and coloured, stone
has a natural beauty unnoticed in the West. In former days
Chinese families would have their own stone or 'chop'. They
would carve their name on its base, their emblem on its crest,
dip it in ink and use it for signature. Nowadays such behaviour
could be dangerously pretentious, but the shopkeeper will still

etch out your name in Chinese characters if you ask him.

I circle back to the Public Security Bureau, pick up our visas duly stamped for Simao and Jinghong, and go on to the bus station. It's a four-day journey through forests and fold-mountains to the south – a marvellous opportunity to see rural China. As I enter the hall of the station it seems unduly noisy. There's a real commotion swirling around. Two men have obviously disagreed and, amidst a growing crowd, are energetically haranguing each other. It is strange to see such a vehement dispute in such a public place, and certainly gives the lie to that popular myth, which the West seems so eager to believe, that Orientals have no feelings. These two are certainly possessed of one of our baser emotions – anger – and are giving full vent to it. As I approach, a strange thing happens. The argument abruptly halts. The protagonists and audience move outside as one man, and continue the dispute out of sight in the courtyard. The Chinese have feelings like everyone else, and they're not afraid to show them amongst themselves. In front of Westerners their features may freeze, but their feelings do not. What deep-seated xenophobic insecurity have I touched here to make them hide from me?

I learn something of their anger too. It is not as fierce as it might appear. A really angry man is consumed by his emotion: nothing else exists. He neither knows nor cares who may be watching. In the West, such violent words at such proximity would have led to blows long ago. Here the argument drags on interminably; the elaborate but empty posturing of turkey-cocks. Just as it seems inevitable that the blood of one combatant must be spilled on the pavement, they back off and shout from a safer distance. When the combatants have put on a good show, they finally allow their friends to separate them and lead them away. This is not the first argument I have seen, but not one of them has ended in blows. The Chinese are not a very physical race. I don't think that they are cowardly, they just dislike violence. They realise it is uncivilised and are not prepared to demean themselves. Their heroes are men of wisdom not action. The Western model of the hard-drinking, hard-hitting, sharp-shooting, sharp-talking individual, ready to take on the world at the drop of a hat, has no place in Chinese culture. Deeply imbued with Communism and Confucianism,

loners are to be pitied and violence scorned. Peaceful co
existence is the ultimate aim.

The peculiarly Oriental concept of 'face' ensures an honour
able solution will be found to most problems. It is difficult for a
Westerner to appreciate the importance of this idea in the East
The closest we can get to it is our idea of 'losing face' or making
fools of ourselves in public, but even this is too limited. The idea
of 'face' in the East is bound up in everything a man does. It is a
the root of the Confucian system of relationships, and the
Chinese have developed a myriad ways of saving and giving
face. Cover up your anger. Put a brave face on things. If you
anger is unjustified you lose face; if justified, then you destro
someone else's face, and in so doing your own must suffer.

Laughter does not just express mirth, it covers embarrass
ment and saves face. The Chinese will use it in any number o
incongruous and extraordinary situations. While in the bu
station, at Kunming I saw a Chinaman stupidly leave his bag
in the middle of the floor while he bought his ticket. Anothe
man, a tiny baby in his arms, came striding for the door
concentrating more on his little son than on where he was going
Sent flying by the bags, he saved his son only by twisting round
in mid air like an acrobat, to crash down on his side. For a
second his face was contorted with rage. A man at the counter
looked at him and started to giggle. Such laughter would have
provoked me to fury, but the father knew what it meant. He se
his features and headed once again for the door.

If a man steals your face, you may never see him again. If a
man destroys his own face he may never want to see anyone
again. When I was in Sumatra some Japanese engineers were
damming a crater lake. The retaining wall was faulty. There
was a small defect in the plans. That night the architect com
mitted hara-kiri. In Japan at least you can regain your face by
taking your life.

I step up to a counter with our travel visas and a note saying
'Please can I have three tickets for Simao?' The woman close
the visas, pushes them back across the counter to me with my
note and waves a hand.

'Dear lady, I don't think you quite understand. Look.'
I direct her gaze to the appropriate part of my visa: 'Simao
Three tickets.'

'Mao, mao (No, no).'

I get out some money to support my claim and push it across
the counter to her. She pushes it back. 'Mao, mao.' We push the
money backwards and forwards with the alacrity of croupiers at
a roulette table. I'm not moving until I get the tickets. There are
no trains south, and I have a valid visa. Why won't she give me
the bus tickets? It is such a little thing for her and such a big
thing for me. For once I find the language barrier infuriating.
Every so often you come up against a blank wall of officialdom
in China. You can batter yourself senseless against it, but it
won't give way. I can get no further than this masked mannikin
across the counter, jerkily waving an arm and spouting 'Mao,
mao.'

At last she summons another lady, her superior. I hand her
my note. She reads it, turns it over, scribbles Chinese characters
all over the back of it, hands it back and waits expectantly for
me to read it.

'Mao, mao.' It's my turn now to utter the magic words this
time. 'I don't read Chinese.' I give her the money. Dead-lock.
She doesn't know what to do. There's only one thing left. I leave
the building with her lunatic laughter ringing in my ears.

Back at the hotel, I show my note to the clerk behind the desk:
'What does this mean?'

He looks at it: 'It means: it is not permitted.'

'Could you pronounce it for me?'

And so I hear the words that I was to hear so often again
during my stay in China.

'Why can't I buy a bus ticket to Simao?'

'You must go by plane.'

'Why can't I go by bus?'

'Because it is not permitted.'

Is he making a joke? I look at his face. No, I don't think so. I
repeat his words in Chinese and am surprised to receive a wry
grin. Perhaps he does have a sense of humour after all. It makes
no difference: these words spell the end. There is no breaking a
rule in China, or even questioning it so far as I can see. The
disconcerting thing is that the rules seem to change every day.
One day you are refused a visa, the next given it; one day the
dormitories are full, the next empty; one day you can pay in
remninbi, the next it must be tourist vouchers. The Chinese

don't appear to notice the contradictions, but they are discon
certing to a Westerner. Where are all these rules? We don't se
them written down or pasted up anywhere; perhaps the
change too fast. How is it that everyone else appears to know
them? Do they really exist or are they a massive confidence tric
used by officials to get their own way?

Though one is sometimes tempted to wonder, there is n
doubt as to the reality of these regulations. This web of rule
inspires fear and stifles initiative. The old in China lament th
fact that people don't help each other now as they used to
People are afraid to step out of line in any way.

On each floor of the hotel stands a reception room to loo
after the keys of that floor – a typical example of the Chines
policy of overmanning. The ground floor reception could loo
after everyone's key, but why use one person when two will do
This hotel is positively progressive. Here you are trusted to loc
and unlock your door yourself, at others the receptionist mus
do it for you. But what if the receptionist is not there when yo
want to get into your room? You hunt for him, but can't fin
him. You look for your key but don't know which one it is. Yo
go to the receptionist on the floor below. Can he help you
'Mao, mao,' he cries, he cannot leave his floor. You make hir
come upstairs for he knows where your key is kept, but he sti
won't help. 'Mao, mao, it is not permitted.' He cannot let yo
into your room, and now that he's here, he won't even let yo
get your key for yourself. You want to wring his neck, but he'
only being careful. When any initiative is open to misconstruc
tion, any deviation open to criticism, it is safer to keep your hea
down, ask no questions, and allow no questions to be asked c
you.

'Mao, mao, it is not permitted.'

It is hard to remember that he is not purposely obstructive
just scared. This may not be a police state like Russia, but it i
hardly less total in its obedience to the Party. He fears the wrat
of the Party more than the anger of one tourist. After the ravage
of the past decade he just wants to get through his day withou
any trouble. Why is this tourist so insistent on creating a
'incident'? That must be avoided at all costs, but what to do
Better to say and do nothing than risk making a mistake.

It takes a lot more explaining, and the hotel manager, to ge me into my room. I wonder if I've got the receptionist into trouble. If I have, I can only say that it's not my fault. It's the fault of the system – the oldest excuse in the book and no doubt exactly what the receptionist was saying to me earlier.

I must not blame them for their pettifogging ways. No doubt they are more acutely aware of the problems than me, but the political world is so uncertain that they cannot afford to take any chances. One only has to look at the careers of the two leading Chinese politicians since the war, Mao and Deng Xiao Ping, to understand the instability of the Chinese situation. One moment Mao is God, the next he is nothing. One moment Deng is a traitor, the next he is a saviour. This is the third time he has picked up his political career out of the ashes. The Party has a short memory and a long one too.

What effect can this whirlwind have on the people? Last decade, pictures of Mao adorned every wall in every street. His face, his voice, his thoughts were everywhere. He was worshipped by the people, but now he is gone. No trace of him or his books are to be found. Now Mao is a dirty word. For those who believed in him the psychological damage must be immense. They've been gulled, duped. What can they believe in now?

We get up early to catch a bus to the stone forest, a fantastic rock constellation south-east of Kunming, whose contortions supposedly resemble the budding growth of preternatural trees. The sun rises above the eastern hills sending shafts of light skimming over the fields. Beneath this shimmering ceiling a cloud lies curled in sleep, a dreaming dragon coiled above the field. Dawn's rays dispel phantasmagoria of night. Swirling shapes rise up to battle with the day and are despatched to the upper atmosphere, vanishing as they go, back to the void until such time as night once more calls them back to the cold earth.

Workers walk out into the fields along paths, mattocks slanted over shoulder, dully gleaming like diamonds in the clay of early morning light. The fields are so large that the paths, fragile and insubstantial, merge on the horizon, as if banding together for safety against the overwhelming green, a green so rich and deep that it resembles a chartreuse sea lapping between dark headlands, a green dredged up from depths of ocean and deposited on the hillside. We wind up into the hills to

a dammed valley brimming with water ready to feed the vegetables below. On the far side, villages with brightly tiled roofs
catch the light, hold it a second, imprinting their colourful
image upon it, then fling it up to us watchers in the hills. The
road is lined with trees. Some are clothed in russet and gold. A
breeze ruffles the leaves, sending a swirl of colour down to the
rustling carpet beneath.

Kunming is the city of eternal spring, but here it is autumn.
In China the seasons seem swayed by geography, not chronology. In Kunming it is forever spring, in the stone forest
autumn, in Lhasa winter, and in Simao summer. The people
here are swathed in the same bright colours as the trees. They
are minority tribes: Ye, Bai and Tai. Members of the latter
forced south by the Chinese 'invaders' some seven hundred
years ago, created a new state called Thailand.

At last we descend from the forest of wood to that of stone. It
seems out of place and time. Columns rise smooth and grey to
meet the sky. I climb to the top of one, risking my hands on the
razor edges to balance unsteadily on a pinnacle just above the
rest. I am the focus of a stone force field. A flux of points and
lines radiate about this point, shadows glance down like an off-
set grid. The voice of a brook bumping its way between rock
walls echoes its escape up into the sky. The green tip of a giant
bamboo arches up to the light, strangely natural amongst its
petrified peers. A balancing rock defies the laws of gravity
waiting for a gust of wind or an unwary bird to light upon it and
send it tumbling into the depths.

We lose ourselves in this neolithic graveyard for a day, and
then jog back over the hills in the bus. The return journey
without the support of the sun is cold and dark. The wind
howling through the windows seems to be calling to its friends
in the fields, and stronger and stronger gusts gather together to
buffet the bus. This, amazingly, the Chinese welcome. They
delight in piling layer upon layer of cotton round themselves so
that they can sit beaming at an open window. Jean-Pierre calls
them 'Harleys'. With their turned-up coat collars, thick glasses
and scarves flapping in the breeze, you would think (and perhaps they do) that they are on their Harley Davidson motor-
cycles. Any price is worth paying for the thrill of dangling your
head out of an open window as the bus swoops along in the

darkness. I'm glad to return at length to the cocooned warmth of my bed in the hotel.

6

Morning Mist on the Mekong

DAWN sees John, Jean-Pierre and myself once again on a bus, travelling through the outskirts of town to the airport. We needn't have risen so early. The aeroplane is three hours delayed. Flights here are dependent on the weather in a way which the insulated technology of the West no longer remembers. We watch two military planes taking off, delighting in recognising the antique shapes of fighter planes which we modelled as children.

Eventually our turn arrives and we file out onto the tarmac. Our plane is a twin prop machine with a capacity of forty people. The luggage (having gone in through the same hole as us) is hidden behind a curtain at the back. The stewardess manages a few words of English as we climb aboard (they are apparently trained abroad). As we exchange greetings, Jean-Pierre makes a dash for a window seat: 'I hope there are no Harleys aboard,' he grins mischievously.

As soon as everyone is seated, the stewardess closes the door and gets out a projector. Wispy Chinese characters flicker like ghostly graffiti onto the Captain's door at the front. From the clicking around us we deduce the message: 'Please fasten your seat belts.'

It would have been easier for her to have made an announcement, but this display of makeshift modernity has an endearing quality.

The propellers whirr into motion and howl their disapproval at being unable to move the plane, then suddenly, chocks away. We shoot down the runway at surprising speed and slice up into the air. We pass over terraced fields falling down the hillside like melting plasticine, squares of green with patterns of irrigation channels, and papier mâché mountains with felt coverings. Flying at this speed and height is so much more interesting than supersonic jet travel, even if it is a trifle less secure.

The stewardess appears again. This time she doesn't bother about the projector but stands at the front to make her announcement. Everyone fastens their seat belts. She comes down and greets us with the immortal words; 'Please fasten your belts, it will be a little bit bumpy.'

No sooner are the words out of her mouth than the plane plummets 3,000 feet, dropping like the lump of metal it is, sucked down on a vagrant current of air which, deciding to leave the cold of the upper atmosphere, descends a silent one-way corridor to earth. The approaching mountains rush up alarmingly to meet us. Hand luggage pours from the overhead rack like confetti, garlanding people with socks and sweaters. The pieces from our travelling chess set leap from the board. I rise helplessly to meet the ceiling and am only kept in place by my seat belt. A child at the front starts wailing, and we wonder if our last hour has come. With 2,000 feet to go, and the mountains seemingly a hair's-breadth away, the propellers once again bite air, clawing us into some sort of horizontal motion. An audible sigh shakes the cabin and people begin to pick up their strewn belongings. The captain wisely makes no attempt to return to the turmoil of the upper atmosphere, and we continue on our way, skimming the peaks and forests, to Simao.

We arrive at a tiny airport in a broad valley under cloud. Being used to unseen forces controlling one's destiny at the automated airports of the West, it is amusing to watch one's luggage being loaded on to a cart and trundled by hand across to the terminal, and better still, to follow it on foot. It looks more like a farm than an aerodrome. The contents of the plane cram into a small bus. We have the normal argument amongst ourselves as to where to alight. This is concluded in the normal way by the bus grinding to a halt and everyone getting off.

We find the hotel and explore town. It has a fascinating old quarter, dirty and ramshackle. Its roofs disdain the horizontal, tilting this way and that, merging, abutting and separating in a hotch potch complexity which no architect could hope to match. Ragged urchins peek from every nook and cranny. Old lined faces stare from the shadows of tiny rooms. A haggard tree blocks the way, and the path makes another haphazard detour round it. We dart down a narrow defile between sloping walls and find ourselves in the local vegetable patch. Although there are a few irrigation channels radiating out from a central pool most of these little plots are watered by hand. Dotted amongst them is the occasional rectangular pig sty, each pig being separated from its fellows by a brick wall of appropriate dimensions, with an eating trough running the length of one side.

We have by this time collected a considerable entourage of children, with fingers alternately stuck in the corner of their mouths or waving about in front, pointing at us. John turns his camera on them which sends them diving for the dirt, taking refuge from the 'evil eye' behind a clump of Chinese cabbage. Thus relieved of our retinue we continue to a long wall, beyond the vegetable patch, whose unusual size arouses our interest. Rounding the corner we find a sentry in army uniform lounging in a gateway.

'Follow me,' I say to John and Jean-Pierre. I give the man a long hard stare as I march purposefully between the gates he is guarding. He immediately snaps to attention and gives a smart salute. There seems little worth guarding inside. A gardener tends a circular flower bed. Orchestral music from distant speakers reverberates in a desultory sort of way. A line of buildings under repair edges a dirty parade ground. No one seems very interested in us. No one seems very interested in anything except the gardener in his flowers. We leave him and head back towards the hotel. On the way we see a crowd of people jostling into a large building, and join them, to find ourselves in a Chinese cinema. It is possible to discover something of a nation from the films it makes. Indians tend to rather obvious romances, Americans to tough heroes and attractive villains, and the British to period pieces. Chinese films of ten years ago were creatures of crude propaganda, but the one we see today is surprisingly good. A man is arrested for a crime he didn't commit. He escapes from jail and spends his time evading the authorities and tracking down the real culprit. At last he finds him, and risks his life in bringing him to justice. The authorities arrest him, but the story isn't over yet. Despite his obvious innocence, our hero is an escaped convict and has yet to be pardoned. He recognises the justice of this, and, after all his battles, docilely submits to the ignominy of handcuffs again.

We catch the bus for Jinghong, capital of Xishuangbanna county, at 7.30 a.m. in deep mist. It is New Year's Day. We celebrate various New Years throughout the journey. London for me at 8 a.m., Philadelphia for John at 1 p.m. and Quebec for Jean-Pierre at 2 p.m. As the day warms up, the mist lifts and we find ourselves in semi-tropical surroundings. Banks of giant fern rise up the hillside; cascades of blue and white blossom tumble down to streams in the valleys; soaring trees, fed by the waters, shoot into the sky, while fibrous creepers, mere prisoners of gravity, hang back down to the ground. These are the strongest trees in China. They support the Temple of Heaven and Imperial Palaces in Peking. Beneath their boughs lives the giant panda in his final home on earth outside the bars of a cage. Soldiers at a military outpost check our visas. We roll on through caves scarcely bigger than the bus, cut into the side of the hill along which our road leads. The 'Harleys' are out in force, risking decapitation as we shoot like a tube train through the tunnels.

At last the Mekong unfolds below us, moving sluggishly with its load of rich alluvial silt through the fertile plain of the valley – a plain ruled flat by the even wash of successive floods of the river. Warm air masses from the southern ocean move up over the Gulf of Siam to mix with cold air flooding down from the Siberian wastes and Mongol plains. They meet above China and unleash their devastating monsoon rains. This deluge drains off the Tibetan plateau through Himalayan folds, to transform this lazy serpent curling twenty feet below its banks into a raging monster, threatening to swamp the valley and all that dwell therein. Though overshadowed by its bigger brother the Yangtse, and overlarded with tales of war and destruction, the Mekong is one of the great rivers of Asia. Rising in the inaccessible uplands of Xiang, it flows south along the longitudinal valleys of the Himalayas in a deep trench through Tibet, a mere ridge away from the Yangtse, but where the

Yangtse turns east and north to dissect central China, the Mekong turns south through the heart of Yunnan and embarks upon a new role as divider of nations. It separates Burma and China, Laos and Thailand, then plunging south in a series of rapids through Cambodia and South Vietnam it discharges into the South China Sea, 2,800 miles away from its source.

If a man could follow a drop of water along this course from the roof of the world to the depths of the ocean, what a journey that would make, but the Mekong's journey is not a happy one. From the peace of giant mountains it flows through some of the most troubled lands known to man. An unwilling participant and arbiter in the jealous feuds of nations, it marks the limit of man's territorial ambitions. Many a time the dark silt of the hills has been mixed with the red blood of man, but the river flows on. Nations come and go, but there will always be rain, always mountains, and always a river running to the sea.

John is jubilant: 'Just imagine. Me on the Mekong. I can't believe it.' John missed his call-up to be sent to fight on the Mekong, only by reason of his luck in the lottery of American conscription.

'Just wait till I send a postcard to my friends back home. "Vacationing on the Mekong: wish you were here." '

I wonder how many of his friends are already waiting for him below.

Jinghong, our goal, lies on the far bank. Kublai Khan nominally placed a governor here, but it took another great dictator, seven hundred years later, to bring the area under Chinese control. This was Mao. Now for the first time, Chinese and local tribes live peacefully together and it is one of the few minority areas that visitors are allowed to see. There is an excellent hotel here hidden behind a wrought-iron fence, covered in clematis. It reminds me of something out of colonial Burma. Wicker chairs stand on a veranda before a shady drive lined with palms. To our surprise, sitting in one of the chairs we find an American called Brian.

He seems unduly excited to see us: 'Thank goodness someone's come at last. I'm so glad you're here. There's something I've got to tell you.

'Five days ago I was walking in the surrounding hills, visiting the hill tribe settlements. Most of them seemed quite friendly until I came to one village a little different from the rest. The people wore black leggings and didn't smile. Someone shouted and a group of men surrounded me. One of them had an old musket which he pointed in my direction. They didn't search me or speak. They just pushed me into a wooden hut and barred the door. I sat there wondering why they had done this to me. They weren't thieves. What could they want? When night fell I managed to prise up one of the floorboards. It was a hut built on stilts. I dropped down on to the ground, slipped through the village, and ran and ran until I got back to the hotel; and here I've stayed ever since.'

He sits back in his chair looking, if anything, more worried than previously.

'Maybe they've never seen white people before,' I venture.

'Maybe the last whites they saw were American GIs,' says John.

'Or maybe they didn't like your face' contributes Jean-Pierre.

'Well, whatever it was,' says Brian, 'you'd better not go walking in the hills if you want to stay alive.'

'But that's what we've come down to do,' I say.

'Walk in the hills or stay alive?'

'If the two aren't mutually exclusive, both.'

'Well you can count me out, that's for sure. I think I have been travelling too long,' sighs Brian, 'my nerves have gone.'

'How long have you been away?' says Jean-Pierre somewhat patronisingly with a year and a half's travelling behind him.

'Five years. Five years is too long. You get out of touch, don't you think?'

None of us having been away for five years we keep quiet. The sun sinks down between the line of palms. The shadows creep forward. Not a sound disturbs the scene. This is a forgotten corner of the universe. I think I'm going to like it.

At this time of year it remains cloudy and overcast here until midday. China is a land of early morning mist. The people do not resent the mist, they welcome it. You can lose yourself in mist. The world recedes till it is no more than swirling suggestions. Look at the 'gaps' in a Chinese watercolour and you will realise the importance of mist in the Chinese view of things.

After lunch Brian (reassured that we will keep safely to the

lowlands), together with John and myself, set out for a walk in
the valley. Jean-Pierre has hurt his ankle and has to stay at the
hotel. The landscape discards the lingering shrouds of mist and,
washed with dew, glitters in the sunlight. We head out of town
passing through the concrete of the centre and the brick of the
suburbs before reaching the wood of the encroaching villages.
Surprisingly, wood is not a medium which the Chinese today
care for overmuch. All their new communities are made out of
bricks. They are more substantial though less attractive than
natural wood. The older villages bake their bricks in the fields.
Their dwellings rise up from the earth, soft, rounded, and
weathered – more the product of nature than of man. More
recent villages have their own flagon-shaped kilns sunk into the
ground, where they bake angular bricks. Their houses stand
sharp and square, bearing the stamp of progress. No doubt
thick brick walls provide welcome protection against the creeping winter chill, but down here in warmer southern climes,
a further factor comes into play: snobbery. The more easily
available and ethnic medium, wood, is left to the 'primitive'
minorities to exploit. The Han Chinese are not so dependent on
their environment: they can manufacture their own materials
from which to build. It is sad how 'civilisation' often seems to
involve a distancing of the self from nature. Nature's ways are
condemned as simple and primitive. In fact simple ways are
often the best, and the wooden houses of the minorities seem
more attractive to me than the brick of the Chinese. Worst of all
seem the 'advanced' concrete structures of the town centre. The
Chinese are most proud of these, yet they interest me least. I can
find them in any urban slum in England. Yet perhaps I am
being too hard. What is most pleasing to the eye is not necessarily easiest on the body. The breeze which is excluded from
the block of flats may yet gain entry through the chinks of a
wooden hut. The Chinese who live in such blocks count themselves lucky.

    Another link joining Chinese villages to the twentieth century
is the power line. No matter how distant the village, the Chinese
will always get an electricity cable to it, like a long umbilical
cord connecting it to the mother. Though I have found numer-
ous power lines, I have never found a generator. I have a vision
of all the power lines in the country converging on one mon-

strous station in the heart of China: a giant black spider pulsat-
ing in the midst of a fragile steel web. These lines festoon the
trees and loop for miles across the valley like long washing lines
on gnarled old trunks or stakes. Unlike our great pylons at
home, marching stridently over the landscape, challenging the
eye in their glittering armour, these lines make no impression on
the scene and are like tatty pieces of string held rather apolo-
getically aloft by withered and weather-worn men. They may
just end in a threshing machine, or a lonely light bulb, or
perhaps an ancient radio, but they provide a vital link.

Our arrival at one of these more remote Chinese villages
causes quite a stir, and we become the focal point of a mass of
pointing children. Presently a man, evidently their school-
teacher, dressed in the usual blue clothing, appears on the
scene, and in a few broken words of English invites us into his
house for tea. His home is one of a row in a low barn-like
structure made of bricks. It comprises a room fifteen by ten feet
where he lives with his wife and four children. Nearly all the
space is taken up by a double bed and a large, beautifully inlaid
wooden chest. His wife brings us tea, and we distribute sweets
to the gathering children of the village who are pushing into the
room. The youngest are too afraid to take any. The village
teacher is a man of intelligence. He knows a few words of
English. It is very difficult to talk, but we are eager to learn, and
he is eager to show off in front of the village, so we try. As a
rudimentary and, as we supposed, fairly safe starter, we say
'China good,' and smile encouragingly. We are consequently
startled by the vehemence of his reply when he spits out: 'China
no good,' and grimaces.

At first we think he is being politely deprecative in front of
more economically advanced Westerners, but it soon becomes
apparent that he means it. Slowly the story comes out. He was
moved here as a boy with his family, twenty years ago, from
Shanghai. Mao moved vast numbers of 'intellectuals' from
Shanghai and other urban centres to the outer provinces in
order to stabilise the unsettled border regions and bring the
minorities under central influence; our school teacher was
evidently one of them. The shock and despair caused to a
cultivated city gentleman who is uprooted from his home
environment and peremptorily relocated in the back of beyond

as a peasant, surrounded by hostile foreigners, with no hope o advancement, and no possessions save what he could cram into one family chest, can easily be imagined. The resentment run deep. This man, though he can only have been a boy at the time of the move, is filled with anger and a sense of useless isolation Perhaps his son, born in the country, will be brought up a peasant and find it easier or perhaps he will inherit his father' anger and resentment as set as the lines on his puckered brow We leave him to his misery, but, ever hospitable and keen to show he has not quite lost his urbane charm, he summons up a smile and a wave at our parting.

We continue down the valley and soon find ourselve amongst minority villages. These are not the savage hill tribes men that Brian encountered, but peace-loving agricultura people. They are mainly of the Tai tribe (or Dai as it is some times spelt), and seem more advanced than the hill tribes o Northern Thailand, though perhaps less advanced than the plains people there. Their houses are made entirely of wood taken from the ironwood tree. This produces the hardest and heaviest of all woods. We find an ironwood log on the ground and, between the three of us, are unable even to roll it. These houses will not fall down easily. Built up above the ground on sturdy trunks, each resting upon a circular stone for foundation they are proof against the recurrent mud and flood. Indeed, the inhabitants have only to raise up their wooden ladders, to turn their homes into little fortresses. The walls of wicker or planking slope gently outwards and are capped with an outer roof o thatch running round the building. An inner vault, overlapping this, rises above the main room like a pyramid, once again o thatch or, in some of the wealthier villages, of tiles. The pillar are joined by a lattice of connecting beams forming stockade for the pigs, a kennel for the dog, shelter for the canoe and occasionally on this side of the river, even a garage for the bicycle. A wooden fence at the front sometimes encloses a garden with a couple of trees, a little shrine and a hole for pigs to wander in and out.

A long sunny verandah runs along one side of the houses from which women stare down at the white strangers, while thei husbands are out at work in the fields. The inner confines o these houses, however, remain a mystery until one lady, slightl

The advantage of long chop sticks

The Chinese have their own way of doing everything

Strip farming

bolder than the others, beckons us up for tea. The people here
are more sturdy and less retiring than the Chinese and the
women less petite. There is a ruggedness about them that I find
appealing. You can separate hill dwellers from people that live
on the plains the world over. The former, like their native hills,
are solid, enduring and dependable. Life is stark and natural
selection ruthless in the chill air of the mountains. You don't see
weak or diseased hill tribesmen. Only the fit and healthy
survive. On the fertile plains the people can afford to keep
their sickly brethren. The demons sloth and idleness creep in
and men are tempted to malinger in the shade rather than
work in the sun. The crops will ripen well enough without
them. In the hills there are no such choices. You work all day
to eke out a living from the soil, and sleep all night to recoup
your energy for the morrow. If this produces a certain dourness
of spirit it does at least breed strength of heart.

The house we are in is one of the more affluent ones in the
village. We go up and sit on a sort of bench, set into, and
running the length of the gently sloping verandah wall. It has a
rush mat for padding. It is all very clean, strong and airy – a
lovely place in which to live. The verandah extends down one
side, the sleeping quarters down another, a store room and little
open platform for cleaning and washing down a third. The rest
is taken up by a large central rectangular living-room with a
doorway opening on to it from the middle of the verandah, and
a hearth next to that. The interior design is like this:

and the exterior looks something like this:

The lady's children and friends drift up the steps to see us, and one of them traipses off to get some water. Watching her as she goes, in her colourful wrap-around skirt, bright hem dancing just above the ground, woven jacket and pointed hat, I realise how effectively the Chinese have destroyed the image of women elsewhere. I had almost forgotten what a woman looked like. Worse than this, I had stopped looking at people. The Chinese have attacked the idea of the individual to such an extent that they have almost destroyed identity itself. Submerge everyone in a monotonous sea of blue monocrome and you take away their individuality. Slap them on the back, remove their name, and call them comrade, and you take away their identity. The depersonalising effect of this doctrine is very disturbing.

At first I found the absence of make-up, the absence of mirrors and the absence of vanity a refreshing change. Now I just find it drab. The people are reduced to the lowest common denominator: dark blue. If one person cannot have something then no one can have it. The Chinese have confused equality with identity. For people to have equal rights, or even equal wealth, it is not necessary for them to be physically identical.

At the root of this question lies the old problem of freedom and equality. Should people be free to differ from each other or not? At present the Chinese are willing to sacrifice their freedom for the sake of order. The West has enjoyed an unprecedented period of nearly forty years' peace. Westerners take their order for granted and seek freedom. The Chinese have passed through an unprecedented period of seventy years' chaos and seek, above all, order. The luxury of freedom is a secondary consideration. The older people who have lived through the long civil war, the invasion by Japan, the Second World War, the agricultural revolution and the Cultural Revolution, are willing to pay any price for peace. They will swop freedom for order. The last few years since Mao's death are the first quiet years they have known. For once they have no fear of soldiers or famine: it is a golden age. But a new generation is emerging; a generation without the memories of chaos of its revolutionary parents; a generation which feels a sense of oppression; a generation that does not necessarily hold equality above freedom. The Chinese people revolted for their freedom, and may find subjugation to the state as distasteful as subjugation to feudal landlords. The pendulum swung back in favour of freedom in the Cultural Revolution. Such freedom, or anarchy, was not to the people's liking. The pendulum swung back once more in favour of state control. How long before it swings again? Mao looked into the future and saw continuing revolution. In true Marxist tradition he believed in it. Is this the legacy he has left his people?

We drink some tea in the house and distribute sweets to the children, but prolonged communication is difficult, and we are soon on our way again. Our path slopes down through an orchard studded with colourful pagodas. The sun's rays soften as they melt through the interlocking branches to dapple the ground with hazy splodges of light and shade. We descend through ferns to the valley floor. On one side is a lake covered in algae like a mottled green carpet. Were it not for the ducks tracing patterns on it, one might try to walk across its surface. Channels of clear water mark the ducks' progress through space and time. No word or sound disturbs the stillness of the lake. Beyond this in a grove graze some cows, the first I have seen in China. They probably belong to the minorities.

Before us spreads the valley, huge and fertile, a patchwork of colours. Amongst the vegetable crops rise glades of trees. Clumps of reeds thrust up from the river. Wild bamboo shoots rival the cultivated sugar-cane, and ferns vie for attention with giant yellow sunflowers. Every inch of this would be turned under the plough in central China, but in this tropical greenhouse the people can afford to be more dilatory. They do not need to fight to survive. They have merely to channel the abundance of nature into patterns. Life is easy under the sun. Long diagonal paths disappear into the distance. Whole villages are swallowed up in the immensity of the valley floor.

The main body of the Mekong River flows north–south,

cutting across the east end of the valley. The valley itself has been formed by a tributary coming in from the west. Had nature shaped the land slightly differently, this could have been a great river in its own right, flowing southwards to the sea, but its course coincides with the Mekong, so it remains a vassal, unknown save to the villagers of this valley.

Where our path meets the bank, a wire crosses the river. Attached to this by two metal rings and some rope is a boat in which stands an old man with a long stick. We board his flat-bottomed vessel and he punts us across with slow deliberate strokes, secure in the knowledge of his safety wire. The current catches us in midstream, but the wire holds and the force of the river merely slides us smoothly along on our preordained course. We thud into the far bank and alight safely. How many times, I wonder, has old Charon crossed this river? Of what does he dream on his way? Perhaps he has grown old crossing to and fro.

I ask how much it costs and he quotes a few pennies. We each give him this amount, but, shaking his head in perplexity, he pushes Brian's and John's money away. Mine pays for all. The ferryman does not cross the river for profit. He crosses because he is the ferryman.

We take one of the long paths dissecting the valley floor and come amongst the foothills on the far side. The lower slopes are covered with newly planted rubber trees in neat ranks. There is a Chinese village at the base of the hill which is reforesting the area. China is embarking on a campaign next year in which each member of the population is supposed to plant three trees. This should increase its tree count by 3 billion at a stroke.

As we ascend, the hill-tribe communities become more primitive and Brian becomes more agitated. He wants to turn back, but we persuade him to come to the top of the hill with us for a view over the valley. The villages we pass through are becoming distinctly unfriendly. Hostile glares replace the welcoming smiles we received further down. Some of the men-folk carry long smooth-bore flintlock muskets over their shoulders, beautifully inlaid with metal. I've never seen one outside a museum before. When they go off, the whole valley reverberates with the force of the explosion. Fortunately none have ever been pointed in our direction at such a moment. We pass a group of brown-skinned men on the trail, with black leggings and equally dark visages. Brian becomes upset.

'It's them. They're the ones who captured me, I'm sure of it.' I think they are members of the Black Lahu tribe. Away from home, however, and confronted by three whiteskins, they do nothing more than scowl and pass us by. After this, we take a short cut off the track through saplings to the top of the hill, and descend the other side back into the valley.

We are only about forty miles from the Laotian and Burmese borders here. Geographically and sociologically speaking the whole of Burma, North Thailand, South China, Laos, and North Vietnam is one region: it should be called hill-tribe territory. The tribes here are no different to the ones I saw in North Thailand. They drift in a semi-nomadic way across the borders. In one sense the political borders are meaningless, but in another, they are full of significance. If you step on the wrong side of one of them, you may never come back. It is a shame that such a beautiful land should be so unsettled.

The sun sinks behind the western hills as we make our way back across the valley floor to Jinghong. The old ferryman is waiting for us.

Early in the misty morning following I make my way down to the market place to get my boots repaired. No matter how early you get up in China the market place is always busy by the time you arrive. Cobblers are never difficult to find, sitting on the pavement with the pincers, hammers, razors, nails and needles that form the tools of their trade. As I look around me the thought strikes me that I'm faced with a load of old cobblers. I approach one sitting on a corner and start to take off my boots. They're very down at heel and need building up. An English cobbler would laugh and throw them in the bin but by Chinese standards they are good for a few years yet. These people waste nothing. The cobbler whips out a tiny stool, three inches tall, for me to sit on and a piece of newspaper for my feet. Privileged treatment. Immediately a crowd gathers, laughing and smiling at the round-eyed giant perched precariously on his pedestal. The cobbler deftly builds up the heels with strips of rubber from an old tyre, which he nails on and trims off. It is marvellous how a piece of apparently useless old refuse can be made to serve a new purpose and return a worn-out boot to tiptop condition. It is typical of Chinese makeshift ingenuity. The cobbler takes much pride in his work and hands the boots back to me with a flourish. The crowd waits expectantly as I try them on and gives a cheer when I signal my satisfaction. The cobbler looks thoroughly embarrassed by now and I'm sure would be quite happy to disappear off into the crowd without further ado, but we must finish the show or the audience will be disappointed. I give him a few coins in payment. He hands one back, and I leave the stage to a ripple of applause. I hope I don't flatter myself if I say that perhaps he has just reached the high spot of his cobbling career.

When the mist lifts, Brian and I set off again into the valley. This time we stay on the valley floor without venturing into the surrounding hills. The settlements here are larger and more substantial than the ones in the hills. A further feature which sets these tribal villages apart from Chinese ones is the presence of temples. Mao abolished religion. Closer to Jinghong the village temples are mostly disused or used as granaries, but further away, they are still devoted to the gods. The temples are tall wooden halls supported by massive trunk-like central pillars and a network of beams, with aisles down either side. They are easily the biggest buildings in the villages. Each one has an immensely tall bamboo pole arching up into the sky outside, from which flutters a long white streamer, almost to the ground. Unlike the prayer flags of Ladakh, these do not have holy sayings written upon them, but are plain white or embroidered with a simple pattern. Inside some of the temples further streamers hang down in great lengths from the ceiling and paper flowers adorn the altar. Perhaps there has been a festival recently. Though there is normally some sort of raised dais or enclosed altar, there is never any image of the Buddha or any other god. Some of the richer temples are painted a dull red inside, and the pillars decorated with faded gold. Occasionally pottery dragons adorn the lintels and tiles cover the roof. In the corner of each hangs a large tubular hide drum five feet or so in circumference, often with a smaller one next to it, presumably to summon the people to the temple. Although most of the temples are rather dusty and in need of repair, some show signs of recent restoration. Some are used as granaries, whether as an addition or alternative to their religious function I do not know, yet they remain open. No one steals from the gods. I get a strange feeling wandering through these dark, dusty halls. They have a musty smell: cool and soothing after the blaze of the sun. Intrinsically peaceful, places of worship have an aura that sets them apart from other buildings. It is as if the walls and floor, knowing no scenes of strife or anger, emanate serenity. Even amongst the grain, the mind is naturally soothed. These are places of contemplation.

In the court outside one temple, young girls spread out the rice crop with wide-teethed wooden rakes, to bake in the sun. With the other end of their rakes they beat off the stray pigs and chickens, who are always on the lookout for a free guzzle. Outside other older women are milling fluffy white cotton. The ground is white with soft wispy clouds.

Further on we come upon a village hidden in a circle of trees, completely deserted: a ghost town. The houses, though in need of minor repairs, are perfectly sound. It looks as if the population has been spirited away overnight. There is not a sign of life anywhere. What can be the cause of this? Have the people moved on? Was the village ill-fated? Was it struck by plague? Were the people driven off by rivals? Will they return? Who knows?

We go back through fields of sweet potatoes and yams, for dinner. With all these different vegetables about, together with cows and chickens, it seems unnecessary for the food here to be quite as bad as it is.

After a few days walking with us, Brian's nerves seem quite restored, and he decides to go back to Simao. Jean-Pierre's foot, by contrast, shows no sign of improvement, and he is confined, muttering French blasphemies, to the hotel.

7

Pig Country:
Ganenbang

EARLY next morning Brian catches his bus north while John and I go to the river, hoping to catch a boat south to the Burmese border. We have heard that a paddle steamer goes down to a place called Ganenbang or Gungerbahn, (depending on whom you listen to) which we can't find on the map, twice a week. We think it goes today, early, but precisely when and from where it leaves remains a matter of conjecture. We scramble down the bank on to the mud flats and make our way over the stones upstream. Near the bridge a jetty juts out into the river. It is unfortunately deserted, but as it is the only place we have come upon so far where a boat could possibly moor, we sit down on the end of it. By 8 a.m. there is still no sign of life on the river, and we begin to feel that the chances of the boat existing at all, let alone our catching it, are pretty remote. As this thought strikes us, a wisp of smoke appears in the sky beyond the bend, and a faint chugging noise reaches our ears. These heralds are soon joined by the boat itself steaming downstream at a surprising rate with the force of the current behind it. It is two storeys high, a bit like a Mississippi paddle boat, and packed full of people. Obviously we have been waiting at the wrong place. Despite our precarious shouting and gesticulating from the unstable end of the jetty, the boat steams relentlessly past. Just as we give up all hope, however, it turns sharply into the current, and moves upstream to collect us. There's no question of mooring up. As soon as the prow nudges the jetty, we leap aboard. All the seats are full, so I stand up on the roof of the steamer. The plain is quickly left behind, and we are soon twisting our way amongst the hills. Mist swirls around me. I have an impression of thickly wooded slopes plunging down either side to the river. Ghostly trees steam atop murky ridges. The dull thud of the engines tingles up through my toes. I am washed down on Himalayan waters to tropical jungles. The river flows on through Burma, Laos, Thailand, Vietnam, to the sea. I shall flow with it if I can persuade anyone to take me.

Most of the people on the boat are Chinese, although there are a few tribesmen. These are dropped off on various lonely sandbanks along the way. The helmsman has to be careful. The river is shallow and swirling and short of water at this time of year. There is nothing to see in the mist, so I go downstairs and take the seat of one of the departed tribesmen. Two hours later we are in Ganenbang. Everyone gets off, and the clatter of the engines ceases. The silence throbs for a couple of seconds. This is the end of the line.

The river bank is some fifteen feet tall here, and a sloping ramp cut into it leads up to the village. Although there are some wooden houses on stilts on the outskirts, it is essentially a Chinese brick village, with the usual long, low, farm-like buildings, and ridiculously broad mud roads, along which cars will never run. There is a wooden temple overlooking the river. Perhaps the Chinese took this site over from the tribesmen.

Our first problem is finding somewhere to stay. We march through the gateway of the biggest building in the town and find ourselves in a sort of courtyard, enclosed on three sides by long low buildings punctuated at regular intervals by doorways. Separate from this, and partly closing the fourth side, stands a house. For want of a better idea we head for this and find a woman with three children inside. We hand her various notes asking if we can stay the night and she nods her head vigorously and motions us to sit down. This is extremely fortunate. There is no question of showing her our travel visa or any other such formalities (which of course we couldn't do) and she is obviously delighted to have us. She bustles off to get some tea. The three of us sit and drink it, watching the children play on the floor. After an hour the children are still playing, the lady is still pouring tea, and we are beginning to wonder what our next move should be. Perhaps there has been a misunderstanding and she can't give us beds after all. We pretend we want to go to sleep, to see what sort of reaction this will bring. She nods vigorously once again and leads us off to a room in one of the wings of the courtyard. It's rather dusty and derelict, but there are rough quilts on the beds and for 60 fen (20p) one can't complain. There was once apparently some semblance of glass in the one window looking out on the street. Only a few shards remain now, like shark's teeth around the window pane, and the rough sacking draped over it does little to keep out the breeze. In some extraordinary fashion, the walls don't seem to meet the vaulted wooden roof. The partition walls are cut off square, leaving a great triangle of space beneath the roof. This does not worry me overmuch. More disturbing is the fact that I fail to find any point of contact between the roof and the side walls. The roof hovers in some magical fashion a few feet above the rest of the building, providing spacious gaps for the wind to gust through, which it does with great regularity.

There is a saving feature, however, one small concession to the needs of her guests concerning which the proprietress can congratulate herself on providing luxury accommodation. A solitary light bulb hangs down into the middle of the room, on what appears to be a tatty old piece of string. I reach for the switch just above the bulb. It works. I am amazed. Whence comes this electricity I have no idea.

By now the sun has dispelled the morning mist and we set off along the valley. This is pig country. Never before have I seen so many of these snuffling creatures. They roam the streets with perfect confidence, rooting around in the rubbish for scraps to eat, heading out into the fields for a lovely mud bath if they're feeling energetic, or reclining in the shade of a brick wall if they're not. There's one enormous fat white sow with which we forge a particular acquaintance by reason of the fact that she spends her life propping up the wall like a great sack of cement a few feet from our window. She lies there contentedly all day and all night and has never been known to move. John, for some reason, takes an instant dislike to her, jealous, perhaps, that she spends her nights in apparent ease and comfort just a few feet away from the hard bed on which he tosses and turns. Occasionally he will get up, tiptoe to the window, and pull back the sacking to see the sow quietly snoring there, faintly irridescent in the white moonlight. He'll mutter some vaguely ominous threats under his breath, such as: 'One of these days I'll have you for breakfast,' and then return, as if relieved of a great burden, to his bed. He never loses an opportunity to throw a stone at her as we pass by; 'Just to check she's still alive,' he murmurs by way of explanation. Encased in her layer of fat the sow seems quite impervious to pain. The stone just bounces off, or occasionally produces a slight snort if John is feeling particularly vehement. I never quite got to the bottom of the antipathy John seemed to feel for this pig. He certainly didn't have a phobia about pigs. He declared himself indifferent to pigs in general, it was just this pig in particular. Perhaps he found it therapeutic. I, on the other hand, had a sneaking admiration for the animal. I thought it rather wonderful that it could devote itself with such single-minded dedication to the one thing it was good at: getting fat. When that pig passes away it will keep the village in bacon for a month.

Pigs are bright and good-natured and much more useful than dogs. They go around town like hoovers keeping the place clean, are useful in the fields (Mao called them 'mobile fertilizer factories'), and, at the end of it all, you can eat them for breakfast. I wonder if the Chinese ever feel any pangs of regret as they turn their pet pigs into prime pork. There is certainly no love lost between the local pig and dog populations. Occasionally a pack of dogs will set about a piglet and send it scurrying and squeaking for shelter. After reaching a certain size the pigs are impervious to such attacks, but by this stage they are much too fat and lazy to seek any sort of retribution on their canine persecutors.

While pigs may enjoy a pleasant life they certainly do not have a happy end. I was the unwilling witness to one such. While walking one day I heard the disgruntled snorting of a pig on the far side of a wall. I looked over. At first its grunts registered protest that its erstwhile friends should be so rude as to push it over. When they went further and bound its trotters the snorts rose in pitch and volume and the pig grew progressively more alarmed. When its throat was bared, a glistening knife produced, and its captors' intentions became plain, it squealed and squealed in high-pitched panic, producing a frightful racket. It was yelling for help and pleading for its life just as any human would do, but to no avail. None of its fellows could come to its rescue, and as its blood spattered the floor, the shrieks died in its throat and its soul, if such pigs have, escaped through the gash in its neck. The great mass of flesh, previously so frenziedly alive and kicking, was now suddenly and appallingly still. The four executioners stood there. No one liked to move.

Another animal we see a lot of in these parts is the duck. They are domesticated here to a degree not known in the West. There are always plenty of irrigation channels for them to swim along during the day, but towards evening they are herded up by the locals and can be seen waddling back in ungainly processions across the fields, floating a few feet across flooded parts before grounding themselves in the mud and continuing in web-toed indignity across the land. Every so often a splinter group will make a bid for freedom down a side channel, only to be headed off at the next ridge and redirected, tails waggling and beaks quacking in annoyance, back to the village. Why they don't fly off I don't know. Perhaps their wings are clipped. Soon they are all herded into one channel, broader and deeper than the rest, which leads round a bend to a pond on the edge of the village: their very own quackery, a pond they can call their own. When the last duck has paddled in, a little wooden portcullis is dropped and they are penned in for the night.

Quite a high degree of organisation exists in some of the tribal villages on the plains. As we pass through one, a house somewhat longer and lower than the rest catches our eye. The door is open and it is not built up on stilts, so we take a look inside. It is cool and shady and filled with babies. Every inch of the room seems filled with infants, cocooned in cribs which are hanging on straps from the ceiling. It is absolutely quiet. What a good idea. Perhaps we should try it in England. Now all the women folk of the village are free for work. But what are they doing? The place seems deserted.

We have walked in a straight line across the fertile plain away from the river, but it has bent round to meet us again in a great loop. It has carved a broad secondary valley for itself, 150 yards wide, between crumbling cliffs some forty feet high. It moves sluggishly at low water. Broad mud flats have formed on either side, turning to dust at the edges. The water spills around banks

nd islands in midstream, the biggest of which is covered in
banana trees. Here we find the village engaged in cutting down
he trees, punting the trunks across the river, and painstakingly
arrying them up to their homes. It is a massive task. What they
re for, we cannot discover. Perhaps the soft inner core can be
sed as animal fodder.

The landscape here is bigger than at Jinghong and more
beautiful. Beyond the river, the hills march away to Burma and
Laos, fifteen or so miles distant. No transport goes that way.
Apart from the Jinghong steamer and one ferry which crosses
he river at Ganenbang, there are only canoes, and these are
nly good for short distances. Nobody here wants to cross the
border.

We return through groves of banana trees, with the occas-
onal guava and pineapple, to Ganenbang, and find a little
ating house opposite the building in which we are staying. I
eally must have adjusted to the local scale of things, for I find
nyself complaining bitterly at the price of our dinner – 80 fen
25 p)!

The morning mist here is so dense that you become wet just
y walking through it. The afternoon sun by contrast is so warm
hat you can get tanned by it. It seems to be trying to make up
or its miserable performance in the early morning.

On a hillock behind town is a Buddhist stupa made of bricks
nd plaster, and next to this a little reservoir of drinking water. I
m surprised to find the stupa here. It is like the ones I saw in
Thailand, but is made, I suppose, by the Chinese. As we look at
t, a crude discordant clashing sound reaches our ears, strangely
n keeping with the scene. We follow it down to a village
eneath us, and find a procession taking place. A Buddhist
riest in flowing orange robes, together with three little appren-
ices, sits incongruously in a dirty old farm cart, being drawn
long by a tractor. He smiles benignly on the people lining the
ath showering petals upon him. Behind him, vying with the
regular splutterings of the motor, marches a little band clash-
ng cymbals and banging gongs. I am quite prepared to believe
hat I lack the facility to understand certain forms of music, but
his, surely, is beyond anyone's comprehension. It is not so
nuch music as a meaningless cacophony of sound. Perhaps it is
nly intended to attract people's attention, in which case it is

certainly effective, or to frighten away evil spirits – and for all
know it might do that as well. I don't know where the pries
comes from, but he is certainly not from this area. I think tha
he is making a tour of the local temples. This must be a very rar
occurrence which we are privileged to see.

The procession stops at the gate of the temple, and the pries
is carried in and placed, cross-legged, on a mat. The apprentices, being rather less holy, have to make use of their legs. Th
village folk remove their shoes and crowd in after him to knee
on the floor, hands clasped up in front of them. Following th
lead of their headman they set up a wailing chant. At the end c
this the headman offers up a great dish of money covered wit
bay leaves to the priest. The priest spreads his circular fan ove
the offering and launches into a crooning chant of his own. Th
young apprentices have heard it all before and look thoroughl
bored. I'm sure no one asked them if they wanted to come; n
one asked them if they wanted to be monks; no one asked them
they wanted to be celibate; no one asked them if they wanted t
leave their families and live in a monastery. At their age the
can have no idea what's going on. To them it is just a bi,
charade. Perhaps they are right. At last the priest has finished
and the people, with obvious relief and some hilarity, disperse

We cross the river in the ferry and head up into the moun
tains on the far side. The further we get from Ganenbang, th
more obvious become the stares. The country grows very wild
As we ascend we leave the fields and all semblance of a patl
behind us. The jungle begins to get a grip. The mountain
ripple away, a succession of ridges and troughs. If we were t
carry on walking in a straight line all day, we would ente
Burma. The people round here look pretty savage. The ol
women with their leg trappings, knee-length skirts and jacket
as rough as their skin, carry immense loads up the mountain
Two straps round their burdens attach to a wooden halte
round their necks, and from there a further strap loops roun
their foreheads to bring the powerful neck muscles into play
They look extremely tough and remind me of Red Indians.

Eventually we reach the top of a minor peak and look bac,
down the valley. The Mekong twists like a huge serpent, out c
sight, having cut for itself a broad defile through the valley. Fa
beneath tiny figures still ferry matchsticks from a little island i

the stream, and painstakingly crawl up the far bank with their loads on their backs. Somewhere sleeps a room full of babies. Against a shady wall in a village in the distance sleeps a great white sow. Out of sight upstream rests an irate French-Canadian with a bad foot. That much is sure. The rest remains a mystery.

Behind us, and some little distance along the ridge on which we stand, a plume of smoke curls up into the air. I am keen to find a path through the jungle to explore it, but John is most insistent that we get back. We go down the mountain, past a tree lined lake to the river, and back along its bank towards Ganenbang. One could spend happy weeks exploring this valley in every direction and never get bored. It is a hidden paradise in the hills.

By the time we reach the ferry point, it is dark and there is no sign of the ferryman. We shout, but to no avail. I hope we are not here for the night. There seems to be nothing for it but to lie flat on my back and stare up at the inky sky. This is a satisfying pastime. I look at the clear white moon, the object of so much attention from the ancient Chinese poets. It has been our constant companion in the sky since midday. Even the moon and stars, it seems, obey different laws in this valley; bewitched by the magic of the gleaming black and silver river.

John becomes a little agitated so I bombard the opposite bank with English folk songs, determined not to stop till something happens. The ferryman falls prey to my own special incantations, quickly appears, and motors across to rescue us. Anything to stop the row.

Walking back to the town, we are amazed to find the little eating house still open. It has gone 7 p.m., a time when Chinese in these parts are normally safely tucked up at home. It soon becomes clear that this is no ordinary night. Crowds of people are leaving town clutching seats and benches. We follow the motley collection to a field on the edge of town, where the people sort themselves out into rows facing a large white sheet drawn taut over a wooden frame. After much crackling and whirring it becomes apparent that we are to be treated to a picture show. There is a flickering on the screen and an ancient Hollywood black and white film, crudely dubbed in Chinese, materialises before our eyes. It is an extraordinary sensation, sitting out here under the stars, the swelling black hills for backdrop, with Hollywood half a world away, watching an old stilted movie about white slavery and child beating in the West. I don't think that the West comes out of it in a very good light. Where they got the film from goodness knows. Perhaps it is an ancient piece of anti-capitalist propaganda provided by the thoughtful Chairman Mao. I hope they don't take this sort of rubbish too seriously. Fortunately they seem to find the whole thing highly amusing, and the crowd disperses at the end amidst much laughing and joking. John pauses only to lob a stone at the great white sow before going to bed.

After further exploration of the valley floor we catch the ferry back to Jinghong. It's packed to the gunwales with people carrying great loads of cotton and vegetables. It must be market day in Jinghong. The return journey against the current proves long and cold. We find Jean-Pierre back at the hotel. He is not happy. As well as his bad foot he has managed to contract diarrhoea. Well, at least his condition now lends some justification for the use of his favourite expletive. I try to look on the bright side of things for him. He might as well suffer from this now, while he's immobile anyway: 'But that's just my problem,' he explains, 'I'm not immobile.'

There's obviously no consoling him. He's also unhappy about the trouble he's had with the authorities – trouble, he hastens to add, which is all of our making. They knew that we were no longer at the hotel, and they knew that we hadn't left town on the bus, so where were we? I think they knew that too, but were pestering Jean-Pierre to confirm it. We decide that this is a good moment to leave and buy three tickets for the morrow.

Jinghong is only open to tourists because the Chinese authorities want to show us how well they get on with their minority peoples, but they don't want us to get too close to them, or see too much. They prefer to keep us in the town and show us their latest concrete flats, but if they think we have come all this way down to see those, they are mistaken. They do not realise that what seems modern and innovative to them may seem old-fashioned to us. By copying Western designs they are inviting us to compare them with what we have at home – and they cannot as yet be compared favourably. We are interested in things that are different from our own. We are much more likely

Mao put the people into uniform

The great white sow

o admire something with which we are not familiar: a rural Chinese farmhouse, or a tribesman's hut on stilts up in the hills. These we can admire as being sophisticated and ingenious in their own way. It is a mistake to think we must be interested in second-rate imitations of our own culture.

A pretty girl official comes hurrying over from the Public Security Bureau to see us, clutching a sketchily written notice in English. The message is fairly clear, 'It is not permitted for tourists to go out of town,' but we pretend not to understand. She looks upset, but John saves an awkward situation by getting out his frisbee and throwing it at her. She gives a little shriek and jumps out of the way. She has never seen a frisbee before. When she understands what it is, however, she is delighted with it, and runs to get one of the hotel girls to join in the fun. During the course of the game her hat comes off, and a long pony tail of black hair spills down to her waist. Femininity, it seems, is not quite dead.

8

In Search of the Circular Rainbow: Emei

RETURN journeys are never a interesting as outgoing ones We have the usual problem with the hotel at Simao. It wants t charge us four times more than we paid before. We renew ou acquaintance with the ancien propellered aeroplane. A few cows pause briefly in the mids of their munching and look u quizzically, if rather stupidly as we hurl ourselves dow the runway. None fortunatel chooses that particular moment to stroll over to the slightl greener grass on the other side of the runway. Soon we ar banking steeply over Western Lake, a three-masted fishing boa a mere model beneath us, to find the entrance to the valley an narrow strip of tarmac which is Kunming aerodrome.

After booking into the Kunming Hotel once more, Jean Pierre and I catch a bus back to Western Lake, over which w have just passed. It is more of an inland sea than a lake. Fishin boats are lost in it. Even from the air we were unable to see th perimeter of the water. A huge cliff fronts its eastern edge. Ato this, far above the troubles of mankind, halfway to heaven, is Buddhist monastery clinging to the rock face. Looking out ove the abyss the monks had only wind, sea and air to disturb them Free from worldly cares, their supplies were hauled up the cli in a wooden basket.

Today the monks are gone, and a well-worn track leads to th

104

oors of their former retreat. We follow it, winding back and orth up the cliff face. At the top a monstrous grinning guardian onfronts us from the first gate, thrice life size, grimacing ideously and brandishing a sword. Beyond this the path oubles back on itself in narrow steps, easily defensible if need e, to a cave containing the Buddha. The image is surprisingly mall after the size of the guardian, but I suppose size is no neasure of sanctity. The cliff is absolutely sheer here, and mooth as glass. The way to the topmost pagoda or dragon gate s it is called had to be tunnelled out of the rock. The 'gate' itself s just a rock parapet. This is a place of nature, a place of ontemplation: nothing has been added. Man has not built a ome here, but merely burrowed out a little hole for himself. ou feel the weight of the rock above, the depth of rock behind, he airy void before and the spreading water beneath. The cliff, great unjointed wall, falls dizzily away to a fishing village. It is he sort of place where the soul feels slightly precarious, as if at ny moment it might take wing.

Beside the village, and in stark contrast to the crowded huts f the fishermen, is a palatial residence. An embankment tretches out into the lake like a finger, enclosing a harbour, merald-green in contrast to the blue depths of the lake. Jean-ierre tosses a walnut over the parapet, it falls in a lazy arc, the eight belying its deadly speed until it hits the ground and xplodes into fragments like a tiny bomb. It could be you.

Today the peace of this place is rudely disturbed by the click f a thousand camera shutters. An unending line of Chinese toil p here for the sole purpose of having their picture taken. They it down for a second on the parapet, adopt a suitably artificial ose, wait for the click, and are away. They're not interested in he view, they hardly bother turning round to look at it. They re only looking for a backdrop. This place was created that one night forget self and contemplate nature. These people regard hemselves and forget nature, but at least they're happy. I vonder what the old monks would think of all this. Perhaps hey wouldn't mind.

We walk back down the path, visiting two other temples on he way. One of them has beautifully decorated panels lining he walls, the other has a large cave carved into the rock, whose valls are a confused mass of humanity. Deformed mutants with

extra eyes and noses peep out at you, elongated arms clutch a
the air, contorted legs strain in impossible angles, hunch
backed dwarfs crawl amidst the turmoil. It is the mangle
remains of a nuclear holocaust, a surreal landscape of perverte
limbs. At the heart of it all sits a giant cross-legged Buddha wit
the hint of a smile straining the edge of his mouth.

An old Chinese woman bows three times to the ground befor
the guardian monster at the gate. A crowd of youths laugh a
her. 'Surely you don't still believe in this rubbish,' they seem t
say, but she does not hear them. For her, this has been a painfu
pilgrimage to pay homage to the gods of her youth. She ha
hobbled up the mountain on miniature bound feet, the awfu
legacy of another era, an era when tiny feet were beautiful an
their owners never expected to use them. With every step sh
takes, she pays the price in pain and humiliation. It was all fo
nothing. Now everyone is equal and no man carries anothe
Now she is a useless cripple, an object of scorn, not admiration

We return to the hotel, pick up our belongings and catch th
night train to Emei-Shan, the holy mountain. What a contras
this journey makes to my feverish ordeal of Christmas Eve.
spend a comfortable night on my 'hard berth' and wak
amongst mountain peaks. Throughout the night the train ha
been puffing north through the eastern Himalayas. Over one
third of the track between Chongqing and Emei runs under th
mountains. The Chinese painstakingly carved miles of tunne
through the rock, strengthening them to withstand the earth
quakes of the area. The viaducts over spectacular gorges an
river valleys in between more than compensate for the darknes
of the tunnels, besides which the staff are all very helpful
unlike the Shanghai crew on the train to Guilin. In contrast t
most other train services, Chinese trains manage to maintain
warm, intimate atmosphere. Perhaps it is only possible to ge
this feeling on an old steam train. There's no hurry, no rush, yo
are all going to the same place at the same speed. Lounging o
the bunks, or perching on the window seats along the side aisle
freed from the strict regimentation of seat numbers and th
barrier of silence that such a formal layout seems to impose, yo
relax and enjoy the journey.

At three o'clock in the afternoon we arrive in the town o
Emei. It lies a hundred miles south of Chengdu, at the foo

of the first great Himalayan step which leads up to the Tibetan plateau, 250 miles to the west. It is a smallish town but with a thriving market. Peasants bring their produce in from the surrounding villages to sell here. We have crossed over the border from Yunnan Province to the Province of Sichuan. This town is different from the others I have visited. The houses, made of wood, seem gaunt, stark and weatherbeaten, as if they have known hard winters. The interior of the eating houses, of which here appear to be a remarkable number, by contrast seem bright and cheerful. Lively chatter meets the ear as you go in from the cold. Men wrapped up in layers of clothing, with fingerless mittens, dip deep-fried sticks of dough into steaming bowls of soup and milk. The food, too, is different: spicy and interesting with a variety of hot sauces to combat the numbing effects of the weather. The wind howls in anger outside the door. One gets the impression that life is hard in the shadow of the Himalayas.

Our little expedition for the mountain numbers five. We find two other travellers at the hotel who want to join us: Dennis, an Irish engineer who's had enough of engineering, and Paul, an Australian viola player on holiday from his orchestra in Boston. They are pleased to find company for the mountain, but Paul can't help feeling a little disgruntled at seeing us. He waited three years for a friend in the Foreign Office to get him a visa to visit China at the invitation of the Chinese Government. Now he discovers that we got our visas after only three days in Hong Kong. Such, I assure him, are the vicissitudes of life. He sighs, attempts to be philosophical and seems to derive some comfort by passing on news that the mountain is closed due to snow.

Undeterred, we make an early morning start, walking out of town on the road to the mountain. Trees replace houses at the side of the way. In the distance to the right, smoke spurts into a clear sky from a snoutlike chimney atop a rectangular factory. It leaves a grim exclamation mark hovering above the ground: a hint of things to come. This town is about to undergo its industrial revolution.

We visit Baguo monastery at the foot of the mountain, get a map, and obtain permission to climb the mountain. Emei Shan, a whisker under 10,000 feet, is the tallest of China's four holy Budhist mountains. A place of pilgrimage for millennia, its

sides are studded with monasteries, and the Buddha resides on
its summit, at the heart of a circular rainbow on the uppermost
peak. You can see him there, but few go to meet him now. The
stream of pilgrims to the crest dried up a decade ago, quenched
by the tide of the Cultural Revolution. Of the monasteries
those that remain standing stand empty, save for a lonely
caretaker. We set off up the trail to the first one, huge and
deserted, hidden in the hills. In its day it housed over a hundred
monks: now there are none. Torn down in the rage of revolt, it
peaceful inmates, seeking only solitude, were scattered like
chaff in the wind of revolution. Today, surprisingly, the structure is restored, but the monks are not. It stands silent and
empty, waiting for I know not what: priests? pilgrims? tourists?

We pass on over an ornamental bridge with a tiled roof and
little secondary tiers over each end: gloriously unnecessary, but
marvellously graceful. It is a small relation, perhaps, of the
huge military bridges from whose terraces soldiers could lean
and beat down their enemy.

We, however, cross unscathed and follow the stream up the
valley before branching right up an endless flight of stone steps
painstakingly set into the side of the hill, and worn smooth with
the passage of years and pilgrims. At the top is a temple cut into
the rock on one side and supported by wooden stilts on the other
to stop it from falling down into the valley. Religious buildings
differ the world over. You can pass them by and not realise they
are places of worship; you can look inside the door and fail to
comprehend, but once inside, from cave to cathedral, you
always know. You can sense the ancient mustiness of half-
remembered prayer, the smoke of endless guttering candles
drawn into the wood, the smouldering of incense eating into
stone. These timber beams and pillars are darkened with the
years. Long silk hangings weighted down with bronze surround
the silent Buddha; an old man, bent in prayer, mutters before
him. I leave him to his devotions and hurry out into the sunlight
after the others who didn't stop.

I find them three-quarters of the way up the ridge sitting in a
tea-house. This particular place has nothing to commend it, no
view, not even, as it transpires, any tea. The most the lady can
offer us is hot water. My friends, who didn't have time to spend
two minutes in the temple, spend twenty minutes staring at

blank wall in the 'tea' house. What have they come up here for?
The strain of travelling in numbers is beginning to tell. If two's
company, three's a crowd, and four's an expedition, what is
five, I wonder? A catastrophe? I keep my musings to myself.

We come upon our first village below the crest of the hill. The
buildings, of wood, resemble sturdy chalets and are unlike
anything else I have seen in China. These are akin to the
mountain huts of Nepal, only larger and more substantial.
Perhaps the people at work here in the fields have Tibetan or
Mongol blood in their veins. Westwards lies the land of the
Lamas, south, the tribe of the Lolos, and north, the nomad
Mongols. Sichuan is one of the five autonomous regions of
China. The Han grasp on the land is not yet absolute.

We cross over the ridge and down through fields on the other
side to a monastery on the edge of a chasm; through this
tumbles a stream, leaping and bounding in its flight from the
mountain. We have lunch in a pagoda overlooking this knife-
cut gorge, and follow the stream back up the valley. The foothills are behind us now, and that peculiar lightness of spirit one
feels when walking through mountains affects us. The world
takes on sharpness and precision. The outline of things becomes
clear, and you feel you can see forever. Tall peaks rise up either
side, drenched in green, the deep calm green of the forest, not
the vibrant leaping green of the jungle. These mountains are
less pagan than their tropical neighbours, but less stark than
their Nepalese brothers.

Trees jut out at suicidal angles from sheer cliffs, water falls
like silver down the mountainside and lies like crystal in rock
pools. Monkeys crash about in the branches fifty feet above our
heads. Higgledy-piggledy steps, placed here two thousand
years ago, trace a way through trees from monastery to monastery, hidden away in the cool of the hills.

We spend the night in a monastery at the head of the valley.
It is a little tumble-down, but intact still. Obviously the fervour
of the revolutionaries did not carry them this far up the mountain. The first court is largely filled with a mound of coal. It
looks as if it has fallen from the sky, but I suppose it has been
laboriously lugged up by hand. The caretaker takes us through
to the second courtyard, tall and dark at the close of day. The
falling rays of the sun fail to penetrate beneath the tiled roof. A

wooden balcony runs around the upper storey, off which lie the sleeping rooms with their rickety board beds and cotton spun duvets. Planks and sacking cover the windows.

We leave our things on the beds and stroll out to catch the last of the day. The valley falls steeply away before my feet, its slopes thickly clad with trees. The earthen path which has been our guide all day wends its way past with a friendly air. There are no tribes or villages up here. This is the only link the monks have with one another. On a rocky outcrop in a bend of the path, an old man practises his Tai Chi, a sort of slow motion, transcendental shadow boxing, which the Chinese indulge in as a relaxation for mind and body. The more slowly you execute the movements, the greater is your mastery. The movements, worked out over the centuries, seem strange to us Westerners, but the man is unaware of our presence. Birds chirrup in the trees. The last rays of the sun skid over our mountain ridge and pick out some trees from obscurity on the face opposite. There is a shouting and a grating from the monastery behind us. The caretaker wants to shut up the wooden gate for the night. We troop inside in silence and he slides the crossbar through its iron stanchions. Behind these lofty walls and sturdy gates we are proof against whatever perils these inmates might fear. They have coal enough for a ten-year siege at least.

Unfortunately John manages to end up on the wrong side of these various barricades, and it is not until we sit down to our evening meal in the monk's kitchen that we spot his absence. A dull thumping noise comes to our notice, and it becomes apparent that there is someone outside the gate; someone who would prefer to be inside the gate, and who is endeavouring to batter his way from one side of the gate to the other without the faintest trace of success. The gates present a formidable barrier and would be proof against twenty such as he. He angrily identifies himself. The caretaker, on our recommendation, draws back the crossbar, swings open one gate, and allows a disgruntled figure to stalk in, before shutting up, once more, for the night.

After dinner we retire to our sleeping quarters for a little candle-lit chess before the fierce cold forces us to put on all our clothes and crawl into our sleeping bags.

Staying in bed for eleven hours proves an easy task. We

emerge at 7.30 a.m. with the dawn, for a bowl of rice porridge. We follow the path along the side of a secondary valley, leading off from the one we climbed yesterday. The monkeys are busy this morning. We drop down the head of the valley, cross a stream and rise steeply up the other side to a pagoda. This commands a magnificent view back down the valley and offers our first glimpse of the holy mountain itself. Its head is shrouded in mist and it presents a sheer stone face towards us. It wears yet a mantle of mystery. Our path takes a shallower gradient up the tree-clad ridge. The mist rolls down, destroying visibility. We toil up a flight of a thousand steps set into the mountain, and a large monastery looms into view. On a stone terrace before it sit two Chinese travellers and a troupe of monkeys scavenging for lunch. The adults are hefty great animals with thick coats, weighing at least six stone. A little one crashes into grandpa and gets picked up, turned upside down by the tail, and tossed aside for his clumsiness. They are not in the least perturbed by our presence, and once they realise no peanuts are forthcoming, spare us not a second thought.

We enter the monastery and warm ourselves round a brazier. This is a much lighter and livelier building. There is a dining hall, and it is possible that there are even some monks here, as well as the monkeys, though it is difficult to tell. The occupants of the monasteries further down the mountain seem to be no more than caretakers. Here, they sell woven straw slippers which they wear over their shoes to stop themselves from slipping on the ice. They have never seen anyone with feet as big as mine, so they are unable to help me. They are in fact unable to stop laughing. We push on into the cloud, slithering around rather helplessly on the ice, and gingerly make our way up to a cold, bare monastery for the night. A rather unfriendly solitary man gives us a bowl of noodles, and we crawl into our sleeping bags for a long cold night.

Jean-Pierre, Dennis and myself wake at dawn and get under way, eager to reach the summit. John and Paul, not content with eleven hours' sleep, get up somewhat later and bring up the rear. It is one of those sparkling mornings when the world is fresh and new, as if it has been created only last night, and created, what's more, solely for your benefit. The sky is crystal, air bubbles into your lungs and mist swirls like a rising tide in the valley beneath. At this height it is clear to the distant peaks, rippling back ridge after ridge to Everest and beyond. The sun climbs above the mountains, tingeing the glistening white with gold. We are surrounded by an ethereal crackling as the ice-frosted twigs snap in the almost imperceptible breeze. We kick our way up the ice slope through this Christmas country, passing a Tibetan family on a pilgrimage to the summit. They have dark, weather-tanned faces and wear their traditional bulky hide coats, fleece inwards, belted at the waist. These are marvellously warm garments and are normally all that Tibetans wear. Huge sleeves dangle down over their hands, and a voluminous fold or pocket above the belt at the front serves as a safe storage place for all their belongings which, needless to say, are few.

I am amazed at this height to see an old woman amongst them, though I understand Tibetan women often look older than they really are. A child is strapped to his mother's back. I hate to think what would happen if she slipped. Even at this altitude one of the men has thrown back one of his sleeves, baring an arm and a shoulder to the elements. The sleeve hangs down, like a discarded trunk, almost to the ground behind him. This is the only form of temperature control these people have. They do not have layers of clothes as we do. Either they are clothed or unclothed. They are an amazingly hardy race, with an inbuilt immunity to cold. Some say that the dark colour of their skin is due, not so much to the weather, as to the dirt. Over the years the grime permeates their skin to form a sort of protective layer. Thus baths are not only things they don't seem to need, but things they shouldn't have. They might wash away their ingrained immunity.

Tibetans do, it must be admitted, have a distinctive smell. My nostrils caught this rancid scent as we passed them on the way, transporting me instantly to the time when I was staying with Nepalese villagers in the Himalayas further west of here. It is the smell of yak butter, and it is a smell which seems to pervade all the dwellings in the Himalayan range. Tibetan women coat their hair with it.

We leave this group behind us on the trail, and come upon an isolated hut inhabited by a little man with a large voice. He disappears into a dark corner and re-emerges clutching some iron crampons. These are miniature versions of their Western counterparts, which strap on to the instep and enable you to walk on rocks with your toe or heel, and grip on ice with the flat of your feet. Thus fortified, we make good progress up to the final monastery where we wait for the others before attempting the peak. Unfortunately when they arrive, they bring the mist with them. We look outside and debate what to do.

Here the characters of the party become more clearly defined. There are several good reasons for not attempting the summit. It might be dangerous and difficult to find in the mist. There may be no view even if we do find it. The conditions aren't right for the rainbow and we might also miss the train from Emei tomorrow morning. The other members put forward their various reasons for not making the attempt without ever revealing the real explanation: they are afraid. It dismays me that one could spend two days climbing a mountain, and then calmly turn around one hour from the top. I am resentful. Constant dawdling has compromised my chances of the peak. Well, nothing is going to stop me from going now. I don my compass, hat and gloves and prepare to continue alone. The others call me insane, more I believe in an attempt to justify their own decisions than to criticize mine. I am happy to go on. I was beginning to feel the frustrations of group travel. The constant questioning, arguing, prevaricating and procrastinating are too much for me. Now I can get on with things again. Things are not longer an issue. Things are easy.

The snow crunches under my feet and the mist swirls around me. I am in a world of my own: a ghost world, a few feet in perimeter, where only I exist – I and the sound of my breathing. I keep all my faculties about me and a close eye on the compass. Looking out for landmarks and following the bearings which I took on the peak before the mist came down, I push my way through a forest. Snow, piled in delicately poised ledges atop each branch, spills down my neck as I pass beneath. The forest thins, the mist lifts, and I am no longer climbing. Before me is void. I have arrived. An enormous cliff drops miles to the valley floor. All my laboriously gained height is shed in one fell swoop; but one step, and I return to earth in seconds. Magically the mist has disappeared. I turn around. There it is, billowing in great sheets behind me, but it dares not invade the sanctity of the Buddha. A tongue of it spills like snow over a gap in the ridge, recoils in sudden shock at the immensity before it and vanishes like a ghost swallowed up in the void. The mountains march away westwards while the broad flat valley beneath curls around the mountain spur and swells out into the plain. It is a magical view. Truly, if the Buddha dwells anywhere, he must be here.

I turn my back on him and plunge down into the mist, carefully retracing my steps and following my 'trail-marks'. An hour and a half later, I am back in the monastery, warming myself by the fire. Here, to my surprise, I find John and Paul still having lunch – so much for their fear of missing the train. They seem resentful of my summit success. They would rather I had failed. I find their small-mindedness hard to bear. Life is raw in the mountains. The veils of everyday existence are stripped away. The nature of things and people becomes clear.

I realise I can no longer travel with John. This is a shame, since we have been together for well over a month and shared good times. I was the frustrated tramp, happiest travelling light and living rough, while he was the frustrated first-class traveller, happiest with piles of luggage, staying in a comfortable hotel. Thus we met halfway. Since Ganenbang, however, he has been undergoing a slight personality crisis: a sort of creeping paranoia. The isolation of our position, buried in the depths of China, amidst a billion 'foreigners' who can't understand him and whom he can't understand, has begun to trouble him. The constant difficulties and obstructions encountered whenever we want to do anything or go anywhere, instead of being cultural or political phenomena, have suddenly assumed, in his eyes, the appearances of personal affronts. I have been witness to too many embarrassing desk-hammering incidents. He feels the need to assert himself against the world in general and myself in particular. This cannot go on and I realise at the top of the mountain that we will have to go our separate ways.

I am aware that at this rate we will miss tomorrow morning's train. John disagrees. This is my opportunity. It is quite safe to leave him with Paul.

'OK,' I say, 'I'll go ahead and see you at the station.'

I am free again to do my own thing and travel at my own speed. I feel quite indefatigable. On the way up I enjoyed the view, on the way down I enjoy the exercise. Taking my crampons off, I roar down the mountain, glissading along the icy slopes on my boots. Suddenly a stabbing pain shoots up into my right heel. I fall into the snow and snatch off my boot. A row of nails is sticking up through the sole. My rubber heel patch has been torn off by the ice, though the nails which attached it to the boot have remained. Landing on a stone with a particular bump, these were driven up through the boot into my heel. Fortunately there's not much to damage in a heel, and it scarcely even seems to bleed. I spend twenty minutes sitting on the ice gouging the nails out with my knife, before resuming my descent.

I soon catch up with Jean-Pierre and Dennis. We take a different route down the mountain and make good time. Towards evening we are back among the foothills and come upon a magnificent monastery at the top of the valley. Inside one of the shrines is a life-size elephant fashioned out of 'white copper', which the people of these mountains consider very valuable. It seems to be solid and is a prodigious weight. It has obviously proved too big to destroy. We stand looking at it, amazed and surprised, half-expecting it to wave its trunk and lumber off its pedestal, but after five minutes it has made no move, so we continue on down the mountain to another monastery for the night. Today I have walked thirty miles up and down the mountain.

The next day we branch off from the trail and follow a valley straight down to the road. On the way we pass a hydroelectric power station. It is a very modest one. With all this water amongst all these mountains there is a tremendous potential for hydroelectric power. This is the first station that I've seen, but there are more on the way.

We catch a lift on the back of a coal lorry, pick up our things from the hotel, and reach the station in time for the train for Chengdu. John and Paul are not there.

9

Mountain City: Chongquing

WE JOIN the queue of people to buy tickets, but when it is our turn, it is the same old story: 'Mao, mao, mao. Tomorrow, tomorrow.'

The clerk flatly refuses to give us tickets. The old feelings of victimisation, annoyance and embarrassment return. Hundreds of people wait in the queue behind us while we argue. Of course we have to give in, but we are not beaten. We give a Chinaman further back in the queue some money to buy tickets for us, and he succeeds. Minutes later a freight train pulls up at the station with an endless line of metal box cattle trucks behind it. Guards open the gates to these trucks and we are surprised to see inside not cattle, but people. Although the trucks are already full to overflowing, the crowd surges forward and somehow manages to filter into them. The lucky ones squat or lean against the walls. The others simply stand with endless patience, staggering or falling whenever the truck jolts in its tracks. What must they think as they stand there: 'I am alive, I have a family, I have enough food for myself and children, and enough money to reach Chengdu. Should I not be happy?' The gates slide shut and we are consigned to darkness. This is why the clerk would not sell us tickets. Westerners are not supposed to travel on such trains, but this is how most Chinese travel, extremely slowly, extremely cheaply and in great numbers. It is a practical solu-

116

tion to the communication problems of a vast nation.

I wonder at the contentment, or is it resignation, of the people. They accept things, I suppose, because they are all in it together. They all share in the poverty as well as the wealth of the nation. There is one realm in China, however, where the principle of equality breaks down and that is the most vital one of all: politics. Here the people are neither equal nor free. The democratic ideal of 'one man, one vote', which one would expect to be Communism in its purest form, does not exist in China. Chairman Mao stated quite openly, 'I do not believe in elections.' But the Chinese have retained the ultimate communal sanction, revolution or the attaining of one's political aims by force, and have exercised it in 1911, throughout the thirties and forties, and again in the late sixties. This, for many Chinese, has been their only participation in politics. If, through the vote, they were given a democratic means of participating in government, they might not have recourse so readily to other means. Government would be more a matter of consent and less a matter of force on both sides, and revolution as a political tool would be rendered obsolete.

Sadly, the political consequence of Communism is not normally the establishment of equal political rights, but the establishment of an unequal élite. Human nature is such that large numbers of people living together in supposed equality, seem unable to remain on equal terms. Eventually a minority rises to the top and subjugates the others. Occasionally a single individual such as Mao is strong enough to do this. When he came to power in the fifties, China was not ready for democracy. Much of the population was too ignorant and distant to hold any meaningful political opinion. Many of the beneficial changes he brought about could only have been achieved by the force of despotism. Once he was in control, he did set about heightening the political awareness of the people but he did not envisage bringing them into the political arena. The only part he envisaged for them was the occasional but recurrent and explosive overturning of the established order: 'There will be struggle in the Party. There will be struggle between the classes. Nothing is certain except struggle.'

As a Marxist he believed in revolution as a continuing process and was not afraid of disorder. He said, 'Have no fear of chaos. The more chaos you dish up, and the longer it goes on, the better. Disorder and chaos are always a good thing.' Whether he and his people still believed this after the Cultural Revolution, however, is another matter. Appallingly, the system he has left behind is destined for such struggle, but this is not what the people want. After seventy years of struggle they want peace. How can this be achieved? A Westerner would say, by creating a democracy, thus bringing the ordinary man into the arena of legitimate politics and giving him a non-violent voice in the ordering of his affairs. Without the necessary measure of consent, signified by participation in democratic elections, government becomes a matter of power, not authority; tyranny, not democracy. The People's Republic professes to believe this. This is what the fifth National People's Congress had to say in 1979:

> The People's Republic of China is a socialist state of the dictatorship of the proletariat, led by the working class and based on the alliance of workers and peasants. The working class exercises leadership over the state through the Communist Party of China . . . all power within the nation lies in the hands of the people . . . the state adheres to the principle of socialist democracy and ensures the people the right to participate in the management of state affairs.

The reality, however, is somewhat different. Only members of the Party have any say in government. The Communist Party has a membership of 35 million. The nation has a population of 1,060 million. China has the biggest Communist Party in the world, but it has the smallest per capita electoral membership with only one person in thirty possessing the right to vote. There exist two parallel systems of government, the Party system, which decides policy, and the state system which implements it. The Party dominates here as everywhere. State positions are held by Party members, and only Party members can participate in state elections. Every five years the party draws up a list of delegates, and elects over 3,400 of them to the National People's Congress. This acts through a standing committee, which is subject to the State Council beneath a Premier.

Separate from this, the primary party gathering is the

National Party Conference, at which 1,500 delegates attend, elected by party committees and military units in the provinces. From this flows a Central Committee of 348 members, a Politburo of 28, and a Standing Committee to the Politburo of 8. The party framework is by no means simple and it is not always apparent where power lies. In addition to the Politburo are the Military Commission and the Central Advisory Committee under Deng Xiao Ping. Without doubt he is the dominant figure in Chinese politics at the moment, even though he prefers to pull his strings from the background. In an effort to avoid the sort of personality cult that was built up around Mao, he has abolished the positions of Party Chairman and Vice-Chairman and is dramatically streamlining the constitution. He is confronting one of the fundamental problems of Chinese government: the size and unwieldy nature of its bureaucracy. He wants to increase efficiency and reduce corruption. In so doing, inevitably it is his political opponents who will suffer. There is no room for opposition in the Chinese constitution. Either one upholds the Party line or one is a class traitor. The only legitimate expression of opposition is the successful popular revolution.

Until the advent of freely contested democratic elections, no effective opposition will be possible within the system, and the spectre of revolution will remain. China was not ready for democracy before; perhaps it is now. The authorities may legitimately claim there is government for the people, but they cannot claim that there is government by the people. Only when they can do that can China legitimately call itself a People's Republic. Only then will the Marxist cycle of revolution be broken.

It takes hours for us to reach Chengdu by train where we pick up an immediate overnight connection to Chongquing, or Chunking as it used to be spelt: hard berths this time, legitimate tourist travel. As we move out of Chengdu I see row upon row of ancient steam trains parked along the sidings. This is a railway enthusiast's paradise; a steam age graveyard.

On the train we make the extraordinary acquaintance of an old Chinese lady and her son, Danny. She is from Hong Kong and drips with furs and jewels. He suffers from Down's Syndrome and is enormously fat. He needs constant attention as he is incapable of looking after himself. She fusses and complains, but despite her wealth is unwilling to pay for any assistance. Their appearance here 'on holiday', as she says, is incomprehensible and incongruous. She invites us into her soft sleeper compartment. Danny is sitting like a great Buddha in the corner. He quite obviously should never be let out of the house without a trained nurse. He has a habit of touching your arm, nodding slowly, and grunting something which sounds like Hong Kong. This particular piece of information he volunteers regularly whenever the conversation becomes animated, and is, presumably, his way of joining in. The old woman never fails to point it out, and say, 'Oh look, Danny's enjoying himself. That means he likes you.'

She has a profound mistrust of the Chinese, treating them with that special brand of contempt that the recently 'elevated' reserve for their former peers. They, in return, are happy to leave her alone, being, for the most part, terrified by Danny's grotesque appearance. This, unfortunately, is where we feature in her scheme of things. Instead of arranging for China Travel Service to meet her at her destination, as they would be happy to do, she dismisses them as a bunch of swindlers and counts on us for our help.

Chongquing is swamped in mist when we arrive. The old lady insists that we all travel in a taxi to the hotel. With Danny taking up half of the back seat, this is a physical impossibility. I manage to appease her by agreeing to go with her, while Dennis and Jean-Pierre go by bus. Chongquing for me is a mass of swirling impressions. We sweep up steeply climbing streets through the mist. Buildings loom into view and shimmer away like the vague and sudden impressions of a ghost train ride at a fair. The people on the pavements are an immanent mass of humanity, neither present nor distant, as indeed is the whole world, seen through the screen of the taxi window. We arrive. I open the door and step into the picture. Shrouds of moisture seem to cling to the stubble on my chin. I am back in the world once again, subject to direct experience. I realise how lucky the low budget traveller is without the trappings and the weight of wealth. Here am I, standing at the Chongquing Hotel: plucked from nowhere, set down nowhere, transported through nowhere. I have no idea where I am, where I've come from or where I'm going. The wealthy carry their world with them. They have no need for the real one. I am disorientated (if such a thing is possible in China). For all the ease and comfort of my journey, I envy Jean-Pierre and Dennis out there in the thick of it, fighting on trams, seeking directions and tramping the streets. By the time they arrive, they will have a picture of the city, the people and its orientation. They will be self-reliant while I shall be lost. To them Chongquing will be a city, to me it will be a taxi and a hotel. Money can get in the way sometimes.

We leave Danny and the baggage at reception and seek rooms. My association with the wealthy Hong Kong lady and my arrival by taxi make it more difficult than usual to get a cheap room, but I succeed in the end. By this time the old lady and the baggage have gone, but Danny remains sitting on a bench, oblivious. I take him to the old lady's room and instal him in front of a radio there, before returning to reception and finding Dennis and Jean-Pierre.

'We've had a terrible time getting here,' they chime.

'Don't talk to me about terrible times,' I reply, 'I've had my share.'

'But you came straight here in a taxi.'

'That's exactly what I mean.'

We dump our things in our room and flee the hotel. Chongquing is well named the mountain city. It is etched onto a great rocky crag. The waters of the Yangtse and its tributary the Kialing swirl round about. The Kialing has already flowed over 300 miles from the mountain heights to the north-east before reaching Chongquing. The Chinese used to regard the Kialing as the main stream, and the Yangtse as its tributary. Either way, old Chunking occupied a commanding and strategic site, above and between this meeting of the waters. Here was the gateway to the distant Yellow Sea. Here was an inland port.

Today Chongquing is an industrial city. I shall remember it as bleak, cold and grey with a permanent pea soup fog. It is out of Dickens' times; a city excited by the potential of its industrial revolution, new to the blacker side of heavy industry, but a stranger still to the material benefits it can bring. For all that, it is not a miserable place. It is too alive. Six million people cram on to this rocky outcrop. Houses crawl up the hill, block upon block, storey on storey, roof on roof, in higgledy-piggledy fashion, as if some child has spilled his building blocks down the slope and left them as they lay, crowded together, one on top of the other, abutting, adjoining and overlapping. Yet through it all run narrow passages scarcely wide enough to pass along; passages whose floors have never seen the light of day. The roofs overhead seem to lean together, conspiring to block out the rays of the sun.

Every inch is covered with brick, wood or concrete, and beneath this the rock itself is hollowed out into great caverns and long tunnels. At night the yellow-lit interiors glow out into the darkness. Within, nameless figures shift mysterious crates and boxes, but whatever secrets lie hid beneath my feet I am unable to penetrate them. These caverns are guarded more closely than any dragon's treasure in its mountain lair. Above ground, cranes swing, furnaces roar, chimneys belch and hammers crash, but it is the myriad little noises from the local industries rather than the roar of machines which predominates. The tap of the cobbler, the clack of the printer, the crunch of the joiner and the chatter of sewing machines fill the air.

The great streets cut a swathe through it all, and despite their enormous width are always full to overflowing with people. I am still not used to seeing such crowds whenever I go outside. In the West such a mass of people would mean something: it would mean that a football match had ended, that a public meeting was about to begin, that a demonstration was taking place. Perhaps if all the tube trains and cars in Central London broke down at half past five on a Friday afternoon and all the workers were made to walk home, one would gain some idea of what it is like to walk in a Chinese town. All the travellers are above ground, and all the streets, not just the pavements, overflowing and all the time – that is Chongquing. Walking the streets is better than sitting in little box rooms. I think that the reading, the painting, the mahjong, the gambling, the singing, the playing and the myriad other things the people did before the Cultural Revolution, have not yet returned. Perhaps people are still scared to enjoy themselves.

We explore the city by day and intend to go to the theatre at night. Unfortunately the old woman gets wind of this and wants us to take her and Danny along too. Come evening, we have to wait for her at reception. She and Danny arrive with ten minutes to go. She stalwartly refuses all my efforts to get them into a taxi. We explain that we can never get Danny there in time on foot, but it is no good: 'No, no, no, walking is so good for one, especially after a meal,' and off she strides ahead, leaving us to haul Danny along behind. We have literally to drag him along, taking one arm each, and even then we move at snail's pace. I'm sure he has never walked this far in his life. We get slower and slower until halfway there we grind to a complete halt. He is stuck on a kerb and can't be budged. We have to fetch the old lady to stir him into action again. Poor fellow, I'm sure he doesn't realise that we are trying to help him. It's impossible to penetrate his feelings beneath that mountainous mass of lard. I'm sure most experiences just bounce off or at best are embedded in his outer layers as he shuffles through life, gently wobbling through the bleak turmoils of existence. But every so often perhaps something does get through and stirs some sort of response inside him. Perhaps even now he is feeling some sort of resentment towards us, his unwilling persecutors. We take it in turns to walk with Danny and the old lady. Being with either one of them for very long is more than can be borne. She is constantly fussing, worrying and complaining about everything, yet refuses ever to help herself.

We arrive at last, half an hour after the performance has started. Trying to slide unnoticed into our seats with Danny the moving mountain is, of course, impossible. Even when finally installed, sandwiched between the old lady and Danny, my problems are not over. To my own and everyone else's annoyance, the old lady keeps turning round to me and explaining what's going on. Danny, on the other hand, largely ignores me, stirring himself occasionally to kick me on the shin. At first I thought this must have been an accident, but after the second kick, I realise with astonishment that it is not clumsiness, but rather a certain nimbleness at work here. Whether this is retribution for dragging him here in the first place, or for unwillingly dominating his mother's attention, I am not quite sure. I try to bury myself in the play, but to no avail; these unwarranted interruptions from either side are enough to keep me in my own world rather than the stage world of make-believe. There is unreality enough all around without refuge in this. I see, however, enough to realise that it is an excellent production, which in other circumstances I would have enjoyed tremendously. It is a favourite Chinese folk tale called *Journey to the West*, in which a Chinese monk travels to India to bring back some ancient Buddhist texts. On his return journey he is beset by various fantastic distractions, but his guardian servants, a bear, a monkey and a pig, protect him from all evil forces and bring him and his holy manuscripts safely home. The animal character-isations, the costumes, the acrobatics and all the special effects are marvellously managed. Peking opera is tremendous fun.

After the play we confidently wait for the old woman to telephone the hotel for a taxi, but she has no intention of doing so; with a cry of 'The night air is so lovely, why don't we walk back to the hotel,' she strides off ahead, leaving us to do our best with Danny. What she is doing touring China with a 'mongo-loid' son, goodness only knows. I'm sure neither of them can enjoy it. I can't help thinking there's more to this than meets the eye.

I go out to buy some provisions for our journey down the river and, on the way, discover an art gallery. This is fascinating, for it is the first gallery I have found since coming to China. It is the first art of any description I have come across in this country. There are some impressionist and oil paintings on display, as well as traditional watercolours. Some of them are extremely good, though mixed with a smattering of crude and ugly Soviet-type poster work, full of iron-faced workers and flag-bearing soldiers. Irrespective of quality, however, they are all surrounded by dirty, broken and cracked wooden frames. It is obvious that no trouble has been taken over their display, yet the Chinese can be so painstaking over such things. Here the pictures seem to have been treated almost with disdain, as if to show that the People's Republic has more important things to worry about than works of art.

This is the legacy of the Cultural Revolution, when art, literature, and all forms of intellectual or leisure activity were condemned as individualistic and bourgeois. People still fear to spend time on such things. So much has been destroyed that it is now impossible to find any art, except in a few Friendship Stores, carefully displayed for foreign guests. The silk costumes of the actors last night were gorgeous, but it is impossible to find anything like them in the shops. Perhaps nobody can afford them and perhaps they are socially divisive. This is not, after all, a consumer society.

Chairman Mao declared: 'There is no such thing as art for art's sake. All our literature and art are for the masses of the people – they are created for the workers, peasants and soldiers, and are for their use.' Such are the words of a soldier who only considers the practical uses of art. 'State' art is a mockery; a prostitution of the real thing. A work of art means different things to different people. If it conveys but one message, it is not art at all, but propaganda. Fortunately many of the pictures in the gallery seem to have passed that phase.

10

Through the Yangtse Gorges

THE BOAT to Wuhan leaves early in the morning, so it is necessary to spend a night on board. I enjoyed the previous evening's opera so much that I am determined to go to another one this evening. Dennis and Jean-Pierre are less than enthusiastic about this, and are willing even to face the prospect of getting the old woman and Danny on board, rather than sitting through 'all that wailing and screeching' again. I give them my rucksack and arrange to meet them on the boat. The Sichuan opera which I see, it must be admitted, is less fun than the Peking one of yesterday. It is a straight play without the acrobatics, dancing and music of the Peking style. Accordingly it is less accessible to foreign ears, and I have few qualms about leaving before the final act to catch my boat.

The hotel clerk gave me directions and, so far as he could, pointed out the location of the boat on my map of the town. In accordance with his instructions I catch a tram and try to communicate to the conductress that I want to go to the boat. We speed through town for some twenty minutes. It seems dark and silent now and the streets are unusually empty. She drops me at the rock's highest point where the road divides, one lane to curve left over a bridge to the far side of the river, the other to continue straight on down to the far end of the promontory. This is a peculiarly stark and desolate place. Why has she left me here? There are no houses and no people. The wind whistles across the great dark river, on over the empty road, and disappears into the night. I walk to the edge of the rock. It drops straight down to the water. The bridge stretches like a long cold monotonous finger to the far side. Should I walk over that? The prospect is daunting. It is not of a human scale. I would never reach the end. It is designed to be driven over quickly.

Should I go back? I find the thought intrinsically unappealing, besides, I think the boat lies ahead, off this rocky outcrop. One thing is certain, I can stay here no longer. It is cold, and it is nine o'clock. Already most Chinese are in bed. In another hour, the city will be dead, and I will be lost. No one will take me in for the night. I will have to wander the streets. I will miss my boat, my friends and my rucksack. This is the first time I have been separated from it on this whole journey. I curse my misfortune and stupidity. I have broken the cardinal rule of travelling: never lose sight of your luggage. It is all I have in this half of the world and it contains my diaries. The rest I can live without, but the loss of my diaries and all the hours I have invested therein would be a cruel blow.

There is a guard at the head of the bridge. Thank goodness I still have my Chinese notes with me; without them I would be lost. I thrust one under his nose: 'Where is the boat?' He looks at me blankly and then points back whence I came. I feel that he, like the bus conductress, must have misunderstood me. I ignore his directions, and carry on walking towards the far end of the promontory. I feel as if I am in a dream: a dream in which I must get somewhere extremely quickly. I don't know where I must go but I know I must get there soon, so I start walking with the sinking feeling that each step is taking me farther away from my ultimate goal.

After twenty minutes I am once more among human habitation. Most of the houses are dark, but men still loiter in the streets in their twos and threes. They look at me suspiciously and none too kindly. The streets get narrower, the walls higher, the houses dirtier. Poor people live here. People who work in the muck and the grime. People who struggle to stay alive. I have a nose for danger and I smell it here. For the first time in China I feel uneasy and vaguely threatened. So far out of my way, so far lost, who would ever know about me? But the road is descending fast now. Soon I will be at the water, and there are lights ahead. There is an open space and people, but, to my chagrin, no boat.

I find myself in a big floodlit yard containing buses and taxis. There are some people in one corner round an official-looking hut, so I bend my steps towards them. Addressing myself to the most important looking man, I try to get my message across: 'Where is the boat for Wuhan?'

Now I enter another dream, Cassandra's dream, a dream in which I have a simple message to convey, an important message, but one which no one seems able to understand.

'No, no boat tonight.'

'Boat tomorrow, I sleep on boat tonight.'

'Hotel, hotel. You want place to sleep.'

'No, no, boat for Wuhan. I want to sleep tonight on boat for Wuhan.'

'No, no, you cannot go tonight. You have no luggage. Where is your luggage?'

'Friends have my luggage on the boat.'

The above conversation was neither simple nor certain. The whole thing, conducted in charades, took on the aspect of a party game to them, which they found very amusing. At the end of it all, I am no nearer my goal.

I try another tack and get out my map of town. Pointing to the place from which the hotel clerk told me the boat left, I say, 'Wuhan. I go there.'

On this point at least they are unanimous and, with one accord, shake their heads. I wonder if they know what a map is? The official points to another place on the map. Something must be done now or I will be here all night. I take the official with me to a taxi, and point very definitely from the taxi, to me, to the place he indicated on the map. To leave no room for doubt, I get out some money as well. The official has a conversation with one of the men in the crowd, who at last steps forward with a smile and opens the door. I thank the official and clamber gratefully inside.

I have at least bought myself a little time. I can, for a period, sit back and let someone else do the work. I am following another clue.

We sweep through the darkness of town, back up the narrow

street, back past the bridge, back, I realise with a sinking heart, towards the hotel. But before we get there, we slope right, falling away off the crest of the ridge, down to the water. I climb out, look over the edge, and see a long ribbed ramp leading down to an expanse of yellow sand, and there at the end of it, tethered by weighty chains and ropes to the floating dock, three great white ships.

Heaving a sigh of relief I pay the driver and head down towards the first ship. The yellow glare of the floodlights lend, once again, an air of unreality to the scene. I am on a stage, walking across the boards to a great painted backdrop. A voice hails me.

'Hey, James! Over here, over here!'

It is Jean-Pierre and Dennis on the landing platform.

'I had a terrible time getting here,' I begin, but Dennis cuts me short.

'That can be nothing to what we've been going through. Listen . . .'

All the while Jean-Pierre is describing short circles round about, muttering: 'Holy cow, she's crazy, crazy man. Something wrong upstairs,' he points to his temple, 'crazy man, Holy cow.'

I home-in again on Dennis: '– so after she insulted the hotel clerk, she started on the taxi driver, screaming and shouting and refusing to give him any money. Well, of course a crowd immediately began to gather round us on the pavement. The Chinese love a scene. Within minutes we were surrounded ten deep on every side, so what does she start to do then? She begins yelling at the crowd, goes straight up to one and tries to shove him away.'

'And do you know what he said,' chimes in Jean-Pierre, 'he just stood right there and said "It is our custom to watch such things, so we will watch." Man, when I found that out it almost killed me.'

'Anyway,' continues Dennis, 'we finally managed to shut her up and bundle her into the car, though we had to pay for the taxi. Now it turns out that the boat is delayed. It won't leave tomorrow. We can't stay on it tonight and we can't go back to the Chongquing Hotel after what she's done. There's a man here from China Travel Service who speaks a little English and

who says we can stay in another hotel, but she's already called
him a swindler and a cheat, and refuses to have anything to do
with him. Now we can't move her at all.'

'Well, we'll have to go to the other hotel, and just ignore
anything she says,' I conclude.

I go over to the man from China Travel Service and explain
to him that the old lady and Danny are a little bit mad, that he's
not to take any notice of anything she says, that we aren't
connected with her, but that we'd all like to spend the night in
the other hotel. Miraculously, two taxis appear and we are
whisked off, though I of course have to travel in the same taxi
as Danny and the old lady, who is wailing and wheedling
throughout. She refuses to move without at least one of us. All
this is interspersed with sickening attempts to appear charming
and amusing. Why does she bother? We know what she's really
like. In vain I plead with her to get China Travel Service to
assist her, as they are only too willing and able to do. No, no,
they are cheats, all of them, they are all against her. Oh, I don't
know them like she does. She knows what they are really like,
but it is all right now, since we, her friends, can help her.

I try to explain that our plans may be different from hers and
that we are not spending our holiday with her, but she refuses to
accept this, and manages to extort a promise that we will not
catch the boat tomorrow without her.

On arrival at the hotel I dive for cover with the others. At all
costs we must avoid being associated with her. After she has
had her row with the staff and left (three of them leading Danny
behind and grinning) we start negotiating for our room. Fortunately they regard them both as mad, so our chances of
getting a cheap room are not too badly prejudiced. Unfortunately our room is next to theirs, and Jean-Pierre refuses to go
up for at least an hour. He seems to have had particularly heavy
exposure to the old lady and refuses to risk the chance of even
passing her in the corridor.

'I will be ill,' he assures us, 'if I so much as set eyes on her.'
Dennis is of a like mind, so we ask the staff, one of whom speaks
a little English and French, if there is anywhere we can wait. To
our amazement he says: 'Yes, would you like to come to the
bar?'

We follow him down to the cellars where he fumbles with his

huge ring of keys, selects the appropriate one, turns the lock, and swings back the door. It is like entering Aladdin's cave. There are rows of rice wines and beers on the shelf, a bar and stools, soft lighting and a music system.

'What'll it be?' he asks.

He even knows the jargon. Soon the old lady and the boat trip are a million miles away, and we drift off to bed on a wave of warmth and jollity.

Getting Danny and the old lady installed in the boat is all the nightmare we expected it to be, but at last it is finished and we can sit back in the knowledge that there is nothing more to do. Now we wait as the Himalayan waters wash us down to the sea.

The major problem which occupies our minds is where to sit. There are four classes of accommodation on board: second, third, fourth and fifth. First class has been abolished as a wicked bourgeois invention. Perhaps classes 2, 3, 4 and 5 are less socially divisive. Our chief priority is dividing ourselves from the society of Danny and the old lady. They travel second class while we travel third class but, as tourists, we are all allowed to use the glass fronted observation lounge in the prow of the ship. This is, without doubt, the best place from which to watch the river but it is, equally without doubt, the place where one is most likely to meet the dreadful duo.

The first day we enter the mighty gorges, known by the Chinese as the throat of the Yangtse. Huge cliffs rise up sheer on either side. In former times the Yangtse used to pour through here and lose itself in a giant swamp beyond. Now the people have tamed the river, building dykes and overflow channels on the plains in an attempt to keep the monster within bounds. In the gorges they have been busy blasting and dredging to make safe passage for the river traffic. Formerly travellers took their lives in their hands when voyaging by river, but it was the only direct route through the mountains. In Marco Polo's time boats would be hauled upstream by lines of coolies, while one brave navigator remained on board, pitting his wits against the demon of the river.

The old lady has decided to capture the scenes on film. As it can get quite dark in the depths of the gorges, she stands up against the window and uses the flash on her camera. Jean-Pierre, in a moment of rare charity, tries to explain that the flash won't help in these circumstances, and that all she will get is it reflection off the glass. She rounds on him: 'Why do you say these things to me? Why do you try to upset me?'

Jean-Pierre reverts to his normal tactic of leaving well alone but it is not so easy this time. Determined to get some use out of her camera, she tries to line us up in front of the window for a photograph.

'I'm not moving,' says Jean-Pierre from the depths of his chair.

'Oh come now, just one little photo to remember you by,' she wheedles.

'No.'

'Just one little photo of my friends,' she persists.

'We're not your friends,' says Jean-Pierre.

He has obviously had enough, and changed tactic to the direct approach. The old lady goes wailing off down the corridor, leaving Danny behind her. Now I have an inkling of how some of the Chinese peasants whom John tried to photograph must have felt. I really didn't want the old lady to photograph me, not through any fear of losing my soul, but because I didn't want such a person to have any part of me.

'Poor old boy,' says Jean-Pierre amicably to Danny, 'I'd be mad too if I had to live with her.'

We build up quite an affection for Danny over the days. As he sits like a great figurehead at the front of the boat, the mystery surrounding him deepens. We meet an American lady on board who teaches English in Chengdu. She is certain she has seen Danny there, wandering the streets without the old lady. Has she returned perhaps to rescue him from the People's Republic?

The scenery is dramatic. Hairline paths zigzag up the steep slopes to villages high above, teeter along the crest, and then spill down again to solitary houses perched on the bank between cliff and river. After two days we come through the gorges to the plains and lakes.

At the heart of China is a crossroads between river and rail. This is Wuhan, the meeting, or in our case parting, of the ways. North lie the plains, west the mountains, east the sea, and south the tropics. We each have our own path to take. Jean-Pierre and Dennis to Peking, Danny and the old lady to Hong Kong, and to Shanghai.

I am sorry to see Jean-Pierre and Dennis go – sorrier still to be going myself, but my time has run out and I must return to England. I float on through the plains, past Nanjing (Southern Capital) to Shanghai at the mouth of the Yangtse: the largest city in the world and home to 12 million people. I pause in Shanghai only long enough to catch an ocean-going liner down the coast to Hong Kong.

Like a drop of water, I travel almost a thousand miles from the Himalayan mountains in the midst of Asia east to the sea, and then, caught up in the current, south the same distance along the coast to Hong Kong and then home.

PART TWO

11

The Forbidden City:
Peking

In 1983, drawn by the irresistible appeal of the Orient, I find myself on board an aeroplane heading East once more. This time I am going direct to Peking, the heart of the nation. On leaving China last year I determined to return to see the capital and the antiquities of the north. Seldom are my resolutions resolved so quickly.

We pass over the Himalayas like an untidy heap of overturned boxes, and swoop down into the People's Republic. Having come down to earth I watch the cyclists on their faintly comical sit-up-and-beg bicycles, pedalling in a very upright fashion at a very sensible speed along the tree-lined avenue to the capital, and I feel, curiously, as if I've come home. A passing Buddhist monk would no doubt nod sagely and declare that China was my spiritual abode. Perhaps he'd be right.

Approaching the city centre I am surprised to see a few individuals in bright clothing, standing out from their monochrome compatriots. I even spy some colourful advertisements pasted up on bill-boards. There have been some changes since last I was here; or perhaps this is just the difference between north and south China.

The streets are overflowing and the hotels crammed to bursting. Though this is a fairly normal state of affairs in any Chinese

town, it is particularly marked at the moment since it is Quin
Ming, the time when the Chinese return home to commemorat
their ancestors. It is also Easter, though few Chinese are awar
of it. Finding a place to stay is a nightmare, but at last I succee
and am able to head off to Tienanmen Square.

Tienanmen Square lies in the heart of the city, and in th
centre of the square lies the body of Chairman Mao in a crysta
sarcophagus within a memorial hall, built in eight months by
million volunteers. When he died in 1976 the nation mourne
and weeping crowds filed past his body, but today, in 1983, th
gates to the hall are closed. No one sees him now. Red Guard
surround his tomb. Beyond, colourful flowers surround th
heroes of the revolution, pictured in friezes on the walls of th
cenotaph. Thus are they remembered. Beyond this, boundin
the northern edge of the square, is the Tienanmen Gate
entrance to the Forbidden City, heart of the old Empire, and, a
the ancients believed, the Universe. Above the gateway, gazin
out across the square from the old world to the new, is a pictur
of Chairman Mao, but all he sees is guards surrounding his ow
tomb.

The Square of Heavenly Peace (Tienanmen) swallows on
up. It is a vast concrete field studded with lights, big enough t
receive an aeroplane or hold an army. In ancient time
Imperial decrees were read from the Tienanmen Gate to th
assembled people. In recent times, heroic speeches were read t
hundreds of thousands of cheering Red Guards. Now peopl
scurry across its surface like swirling spots of dust in thei
agoraphobic anxiety to reach the other side. It was here, on
October 1949, that Mao proclaimed the establishment of th
People's Republic of China. For China history began in 1949. I
has the longest and shortest history of any nation on earth. I
1949 the country lay before Mao *tabula rasa*. All links with th
past were severed. One billion people, a quarter of the world'
population, looked to him for a future. With Emperor, state an
religion gone, Mao was God. He was the saviour who broke an
banished the bourgeois nationalists, and who ushered in th
glorious socialist People's Republic of China. He did indee
work miracles; he was a military genius, and if he had died i
1949 would have been remembered as such. But he did not di
in 1949. He did not die for another twenty-seven years. Tim

enough to reveal the fallibility of his nature. He was an enormous and paradoxical character who projected a vastly inflated image of himself. During his lifetime he was able to shore up his position as God-like ruler of the people. Now that he is dead, and his books and posters have disappeared, this image is fading fast. All that remains is one picture. How long, I wonder, before this too goes.

The Chinese memory, like its history, is both long and short. Symbolic of this are the two museums to the East of the square: Museums to Chinese History and to the Revolution. If, like me, in search of history you go in through the wrong door of the Museum and are confronted by the founding of the Republic, make no mistake, turn round and walk straight out again. If, through some misplaced sense of duty or desire to get value out of your 2p entry ticket, or through mere pragmatism you see it through to the end, you will be too dispirited to enjoy the history section which follows. The Museum to the Founding of the People's Republic is well worth missing. You won't be able to understand much (it being entirely in Chinese) and any pictures which do stray within the realms of comprehension are mere propaganda and should be avoided anyway. Far better save yourself for the Shang bronzes, Tang figurines and Ming vases beyond. Their exquisite shapes and colours help dispel the sombre tedium of the revolution. To the West of the square is the Great Hall of the People, housing the People's Congress, and capable of holding 10,000 men. The square is the product of the state. It is oppressive and inhuman. Man is lost in the midst of the vast grey expanse. He is supposed to be. The individual is nothing; the state is all.

As I approach the Tienanmen Gate, I approach the home of the ancient Emperors. Their dwelling was named the Forbidden City – forbidden to all but the Emperor's family and attendants. This was their world, a world apart, for they seldom stepped outside the confines of their home. The very names of the buildings suggest that these people dwelt on a plane apart, removed from the troubles of ordinary mortals: the Palace of Heavenly Purity, the Hall of Earthly Peace, the Hall of Literary Glory, the Hall of Exuberance, the Palace of All Happiness, the Palace of Concentrated Beauty, the Hall of Preserving Harmony and, at the centre, the Hall of Supreme Harmony.

I pass through the cool of the Tienanmen Gate to the first great courtyard. Tienanmen means heavenly peace, and this is exactly the feeling the buildings induce. The Forbidden City is a succession of huge courtyards bounded by broad walls. The simple harmony of the enclosed space soothes the soul. The buildings do not strive for the skies, like some monstrous tower of Babel, but spread serenely out, courtyard after courtyard like the lapping of waves. The gentle curve of the roofs recalls the lines of nomad tents on the northern plains. The buildings though vast, seem low and cool across the bright courtyards.

If the Great Square oppresses the spirit, the Forbidden City uplifts it. If the Great Square demonstrates the might of the state and the insignificance of the individual, the Forbidden City demonstrates the unity of nature and man's place within it. The Forbidden City was built for a man, for the third Ming Emperor. It took 2,000 men fourteen years, from 1406 to 1420, to complete and, though it covers 250 acres, one feels at home here. The world, however, occasionally impinged upon the Imperial dwelling. In 1644 the invading Manchus razed it to the ground. Yet these warriors were to prove less savage than previous nomadic invaders. They quickly rebuilt the Forbidden City to its original design and showed themselves only too happy to adapt to the Chinese way of life. They founded the Qing dynasty, and ruled from the Forbidden City until the Empire was brought to an end and their home turned into a museum by the founding of the Republic in 1911. Thus the Forbidden City stands today much as it did five hundred years ago, but while then for a stranger to cross its portals meant instant death, today thousands do so daily with impunity.

The Tienanmen Gate pierces the southern wall of the Forbidden City. A Chinese gate is not so much an opening as a fortress, rather like the huge 'pylons' which the ancient Egyptians built round the other side of the world. The gateway itself is like a tunnel, up to a hundred feet long, running horizontally through the structure, and is the only opening the wall presents to the world. Soldiers used to dwell in the fortress above, ready at any time to rain arrows down on to the heads of aggressors. The Chinese were forever building walls and gates and were never daunted by the size of an undertaking. The Tienanmen gate forms part of a wall forty feet high and six feet

thick at the base, lined with brick and surrounding the Forbidden City. Another wall used to surround the town itself. If
you were left on the wrong side of that after nightfall, when the
gates closed, you needed an army to get you back in. Sadly,
what remained of the city wall was torn down by Red Guards in
the fervour of the Cultural Revolution. A further wall separated
the entire Empire from the nomadic horsemen to the north.
This is so huge that it is known the world over quite simply as
the Great Wall.

Peking is the only major capital in the world not to be located
on a river, yet this city, far to the north of the realm, has been the
centre of power in China ever since the thirteenth century.
However, this is not so strange if one looks at the geography of
China. Much of China is mountainous, uninhabited, inhospit-
able and inaccessible. Historically at least, when people talk of
China they mean the two broad river plains of Huangho
(Yellow River) to the north, and Yangtse Kiang in the centre,
together, more recently, with a strip of coast to the south. The
Yangtse (or Changjiang) is the longest river in Asia, and the
Huangho carries more silt than any other river in the world.
The plains which they formed, and their fertile soil, have been a
home to man since the earliest times. Here, nearly half a million
years ago, dwelt Peking Man, the first of our ancestors to
control the magic of fire. The inhabitants of these plains worshipped the rivers. With their irrigating waters and devastating
floods they were the bringers of life and death to the land.

The people were protected by the Himalayan mountains to
the west, the Indo-Chinese jungles to the south and the ocean to
the east. Sealed off from the rest of the world for over 4,000
years, they developed a unique civilisation. Their only exposed
flank was the steppe land to the north. This was the breeding
ground of Nomadic horsemen. In the thirteenth century under
Kublai Khan they overran China and established the foreign
Yuan dynasty, with Peking as their capital. Save for a few brief
decades at the beginning of the Ming dynasty, which replaced
the Yuan in 1368, and at the start of the Republic, Peking, or
Beijing as it is now called, has remained the capital of China.
The very name means Northern Capital. Though not located
on a river, it has been connected from the sixth century by canal
to the sea and to the fertile grain provinces of the south. It lies at

the head of the vast Shaanxi plateau, just south of the Tahaito hills which, surmounted by the Great Wall, formed the northern defence of the realm. Peking was thus in a strategic position to defend itself against invasion from the north, although it must be remembered that two of the three dynasties which used it as capital, the Yuan (AD 1271–1368) and Qing (AD 1644–1911) regarded the northern plains as their home. The Yuan hailed from Mongolia to the north-west, and the Qing from Manchuria to the north-east. What more natural than for them to establish themselves at Peking: for them it was a gateway, not a barrier. It is significant that the intervening, and purely Chinese, Ming dynasty (AD 1368–1644) did more to restore the Great Wall, facing it with stone along its length, than any other. Today parts of the Great Wall and the Forbidden City are being rebuilt, not to keep the foreigners out this time, but to lure them in.

While other tourists catch special buses for their one and a half hour tour of the Great Wall, I make my way to Beijiao market and wait for a local bus. I prefer to see the Great Wall on my own and spend the day on it. A wall which took 300,000 men ten years to build can scarcely be appreciated in one and a half hours, squeezed between breakfast and lunch. On the way to the wall I pass the night soil workers taking their wares in horse-drawn tanks out into the fields. Many parts of Peking have no drains, so, early in the morning, while everyone else is in bed, the night soil workers make their rounds, collecting sewage from the outside lavatories. The Chinese waste nothing, not even this. They do not even view it as a waste product. They call it night soil for that is what it becomes when it is spread on the fields outside the city. In other countries, such workers might be looked down on, but here they are honoured. The people recognise the importance of their work. In the fields green vegetables are planted in long lines next to low mud walls. Plastic sheeting stretches down over them from the top of the walls to the ground on the far side, forming a protective greenhouse. Beside them lie rolled up straw mats which are used to keep the vegetables warm at night. In typically innovative fashion, some farmers have dug shallow trenches for their vegetables, and stretch the sheeting flat across them.

After an hour we come to the hills which form the last barrier between China and the Mongolian plains. It was here, in 221 BC, that the Qin general, Meng Tian, on his Emperor's orders began to build a wall to keep the savage hordes that swept the plains at bay. Throughout its history, China has had cause to fear the north. The harsh weather and barren plains combined to produce the toughest warriors in the world. The Chinese lived in constant fear of these marauding tribes – the Huns, the Turks, the Mongols and the Tartars – which continually probed down into the fertile valleys of the South. Europe too had cause to fear these warlike people. Two of the tribes moved west to form Hungary and Turkey. The third remained to form Mongolia and the fourth, through its savagery, claimed a mythical world for its own: Tartary.

When one man arose in the thirteenth century to unite these tribes beneath his rule, the whole world had cause to fear. Ghengis Khan moulded the 'hordes' into a uniquely mobile fighting force which swept through Asia and Europe to the Adriatic. His Empire stretched from the Pacific on one side to the Mediterranean on the other. He joined two worlds, East and West. No man before or since has conquered and ruled such a vast area. China's Great Wall was little obstacle to such a force. Under the leadership of Kublai, grandson of Ghengis, the fourth Great Khan, they swept over and engulfed the whole country. Such a vast empire so quickly acquired could not stand for long. The empire was split amongst the family. Europe proved too distant and China too close for Kublai. He succumbed to the Chinese way of life and established the foreign Yuan dynasty there.

It was natural for Kublai to choose a capital in the north, near to the Asian steppes of his birth. At first his base of power was his Summer Palace on the plains north of the Great Wall. This was the magical Xanadu of the poet Coleridge. Gradually the comforts of the Chinese lifestyle exerted a pull on him and he moved south to Peking. He it was who brought the town to greatness.

Work was first begun on a northern defence in the Warring States period, 475–221 BC, but the result was piecemeal. Several separate walls were built by independent kingdoms. It was not until the mighty Qin Dynasty arose to unite the land in 221 BC that the wall became a coherent whole. The first Qin Emperor joined the Himalayan mountains to the Yellow Sea along the northern boundary. This prodigious feat was achieved through tyranny and force of arms. Countless skeletons of workers line the foundation of the wall. It stood as an earthen barrier for over a thousand years until the Ming faced it with stone. In its final form, 3,945 miles long, it is the largest construction built by man, and the only one that can be seen from outer space with the naked eye. Two hundred and thirty-five million cubic yards of rammed earth and rubble form the wall's core and 79 million cubic yards of brick and stone its outer shell. Had the wall been designed differently, it could have girdled the world as a dyke eight feet high. It was achieved by man but at a terrible human cost. The population it was designed to protect was significantly weakened by the act of its creation.

After a further hour the bus reaches Badaling and I see the wall like a great armour-plated centipede on the crest of the ridge. It twists this way and that, turning back on itself, following the contours of the hills. Every fifty yards stands a square tower or lookout post where the soldiers could shelter from the winds roaring off the plains. Twenty-five feet high, it is a formidable barrier even now. In Imperial times, it was more than just a wall: it was a paved highway twenty feet wide, along which ten soldiers, or five cavalrymen, could pass abreast over rough terrain. This was important for the defence was stretched in a long thin line. It was vital that reinforcements could be brought swiftly to bear on the points of enemy attack. The towers too were more than billets, they were beacons along which news of an enemy advance could be transmitted swiftly to the capital. Great blocks of stone two feet thick face the wall, carefully laid in layers and mortared together, their fine joints and smooth surfaces providing no purchase for enemy hands. Testament to the skill of the wall's makers is the fact that it stands today.

Hundreds of tourists from Hong Kong swarm along the restored section of the wall this morning. The government has provided a little brick parapet and handrail on the inner wall, though previously there was only the crenellated defence on the outer wall and soldiers stumbled down the steep inclines unassisted. Further along, the unrestored part stretches away east to Shanghaiquon on the coast, and west on the other side across the Gobi desert to the Jiayuguan pass in the Himalayas. The unrestored section is more interesting, not least because it is deserted. In the broken parts, one can see through the layer of rubble to the earthen core below. Some sections of the wall are so steep as to be almost vertical. To the north spread the Mongol Plains. A dusty haze obscures the perspective. It is easy to imagine ancient soldiers in this lonely outpost nervously scanning the horizon for signs of the enemy, and wondering if, should theirs be the section of wall assaulted, they could hold out long enough for help to arrive. A wind funnels up the valley. It was bitter here in winter. I follow the wall along, over a broken patch where time, or the shepherds, have forced a breach; or could this have been the scene of an ancient battle, where wave after wave of savage horsemen broke themselves against the wall, defended by a handful of soldiers above?

I make my way along the serpentine switchback, down into the vales and up on to the crests. There is a cluster of roofs below me. A man looks up and sees me on the wall. Immediately there is a flurry of green-jacketed activity. Soldiers come running up, shouting and waving, shattering the peace. 'You must go back. What do you think you are doing?' they seem to be saying. The Chinese mistrust individualism and dislike independence. They see something wrong in my presence here, alone. Could I have come upon a secret military installation? A path disappears into a hillock opposite. Every so often a dull boom echoes round the mountains, telling of explosions within subterranean caverns. Are they hollowing out the hill? Until recently it was tribes of nomadic horsemen that posed a threat but, now that China has claimed Inner Mongolia as its own, it is threatened by a larger and potentially more dangerous neighbour: the United Soviet Socialist Republic. Mao exhorted the people to build bomb shelters for themselves. Now, no doubt, they will be useful protection against any nuclear attack. Is this some sort of underground base? Is the Great Wall or ɔ more reverting to strategic use?

I try to persuade the soldiers that I am not the slightest bit interested in their present-day military installations and that my sole concern is the 2,000-year-old one under my feet, but it is no use. I am escorted back to the tourist section of the wall. My little expedition was interesting while it lasted, but perhaps I have seen enough. Perhaps I have seen too much! As I make my way back to the road I espy a Chinese lady sweeping the top of the wall with a broom, and imagine a conversation with her: 'Good afternoon madam, and what is your job?'

'I keep the dust off the Great Wall of China.'

After an hour and a quarter, the Peking bus trundles up the road, and, sadly, trundles on by without stopping. It is full. As the last of the air-conditioned tourist buses purr past, I am left in the dust in the side of the road with a handful of Chinese. Another hour goes by. Then an antiquated bus comes rattling up and apparently breaks down beside us. The driver gets off to look at the engine while the people in the queue beside me get on. This isn't a very promising start, but I follow suit, and we are soon chugging away to Peking. The man standing next to me on the bus speaks a little English, and eagerly yet hesitantly, as is the Chinese way, engages me in conversation. He is an assistant engineer at a geological college, and studies coal mining. China has coal reserves of 660,000 million tons. With its massive hydroelectric potential in the Himalayan mountains and newly discovered oil reserves in the South China Sea, it has huge energy resources. I point this out to my friend.

'Ah yes,' he replies, 'but we have little technology, unlike the West.'

'Yes, but while you can develop technology,' I reply, 'you cannot develop resources if you have not got any.'

This is perhaps an over-simplification. It is not always so easy to develop technology. Mao's great leap forward in the fifties, when he tried to modernise agriculture, was a disaster. It attempted too much too quickly. The people were not ready for tractors and communes. The Chinese are now developing at a sensible pace, learning from the Japanese and the United States. But Japan has its own interests to protect. It is terrified that China will become another South Korea or Taiwan, mass-producing cheap electrical goods and undercutting the Japanese market. It will not be easy for the Chinese, but they have made a start.

My friend is on holiday this week, because his sister who is sitting at the front of the bus has got married. She is twenty-three. In an effort to keep the birthrate down men were formerly unable to marry till twenty-seven and women till twenty-five.

Women bearing illegitimate children before that age were treated as criminals, and often sent to prison. Now things have relaxed slightly. Men can marry at twenty-five and women at twenty-three. The government campaign for one-child families however, hedged round by a series of financial, economic and moral incentives, is unrelenting. Demography is one of China's chief concerns, and it is determined to keep its population (currently 2.06 billion) below 2.2 billion until the end of the century. When people marry in China, it is for life. People talk of one-parent families in the West: the talk is of one-child families in the East.

I get my first Chinese lesson on the bus, but am hindered by the Englishman's natural inability to grasp any language other than his own. We have a saying: 'It is better to keep your mouth shut and let people think you a fool, than open it and remove all doubt.' I dislike states of uncertainty however, and remove all doubt.

The next day Peking is enveloped in a dust storm. Sand and grit swirl around the streets, getting into your clothes, your food, your nose, your eyes and leaving you stranded and tearful in the nearest doorway. Women tie coloured gauze veils over their heads. One of them has painted coloured spots on hers, and looks as if she has got measles. Men weather the storm as best they can. It lends the capital an archetypal air. Dynasties come and go with the centuries. The face of the city may change, but every spring Peking is visited by dust storms.

By the time a bus has taken me to the Emperor's Summer Palace in the north-west of the city the storm has abated and the sun shows its face. The old Palace was built for the Emperor Wan Yanliang in 1153 as a retreat from the city during the sweltering summer months. It was first known as the 'Garden of Golden Waters', but it has been rebuilt and renamed over the centuries. The Emperor Quian Long in 1750 made 10,000 labourers dig out the huge Kunming Lake which borders the palace. This was designed to reflect the peace and beauty of its namesake over a thousand miles away in Yunnan province. The lakes and pavilions were intended as places of pleasure and relaxation for the Emperors. This they achieved until 1860, when they were sacked by European troops during the Opium Wars.

The infamous dowager Empress Tsu Hsi, last of the Qing, determined not to forego any of the pleasures of her predecessors, precipitated the fall of the dynasty by building a new palace in 1888 with money which had been set aside to build a navy for the nation. Instead of warships, she created a marble pleasure boat in the grounds of her palace for her own amusement. She paid for it with 5 million ounces of silver extracted in taxes from her impoverished subjects. Her picture adorns the wall of one of her chambers and a very grim lady she looks too, but one cannot resist a grudging admiration for the glorious disregard of such a woman prepared to squander the wealth of a nation on her own delectation.

The palace is a triumph of ingenuity. Its finest feature is the Buddhist temple on Longevity Hill, overlooking the lake. This is a study in perspective. The Chinese were masters at showing you something and then making it disappear – as our foreign emissaries learned to their cost. As you approach the temple over the lake you see, so you suppose, the whole complex rising in five tiers up the side of the hill, crowned with the Buddha Fragrance Tower. Stepping off the boat, the quayside gateway hides the tower from view. Pass through this, and you see it again first above the temple gateway, then, as you approach, framed within it. Descend the steps from the gate and it is snatched from view behind the roof of the great hall. The architects constantly change your perspective as they force you up and down steps. You rise up the hill through a succession of courts and a variety of stairs, being turned this way and that, now looking back on the expanse of lake, now on the golden tiles of an obstructing roof. Finally you climb a great diamond-shaped double staircase cutting across a retaining wall and come upon the tower, but there is more yet. The tower itself conceals the ultimate shrine on the crest of the hill. You rise up a natural staircase leading from crag to crag to the summit, where stands the Temple of Ten Thousand Buddhas. Though placed on top of a hill, the Temple, as a last trick, is concealed by a wall. Tiny porcelain Buddhas line its sides. There are hundreds of them – but not thousands. Ten thousand is a symbolic number in Chinese thinking. Throughout China you will see the Hall of Ten Thousand Statues, or the Cave of Ten Thousand Figures. The 'ten thousand things' means the whole world. Thus here, on the top of a hill hidden from the world, is the whole world.

It is possible to take another route down, through labyrinthine passages twisting in and out of the rock, leading you by secret ways to other temples and other courtyards. The shrines are not so much built on the hill as growing out of it. I reach the bottom again, and follow the covered Long Corridor along its length to the Dowager's stone boat. The corridor itself is a masterpiece of art. Every section of its roof is covered with a fresh pastoral scene. The Empress came here in the summer, so it was important that she could pass from one end of her domain to the other without exposing herself to the gruelling sun. The boat itself, forever anchored in stone next to the quayside, is a delightful nonsense, reminiscent of the follies which Victorian romantics built at the bottom of their gardens. Almost as interesting are the cavernous wooden boathouses beyond, beginning to warp and bow in disrepair. It takes me fifteen minutes to walk back to the Palace along the long corridor. You could do it quicker if you hurried, but who would want to hurry in such a corridor?

Here I see the Imperial Stage with its great wooden boards, and the Imperial Chambers where the Dowager spent her last days. Her throne is so large that a secondary chair had to be made out of cushions within it. It looks disproportionate without an occupant, but when the Dowager sat there with great flowing robes spread out, she must have looked impressive. It is strange how people equate size and height with importance. Thrones are always huge and raised on a dais. The giant furniture and ridiculous boat lend the entire palace a theatrical quality. In a way this is fitting, for the final scenes of the dynasty were enacted on this stage. The Dowager died in 1908. Three years later Dr Sun Yat Sen dropped the curtain on over two thousand years of Imperial rule, and the Empire came to an end.

If you rise early and walk through Tiantan Park you will see the people doing Tai Chi. Normally the movements are performed very slowly in a trance-like state of concentration. Two women I see perform a variation of this with long wooden staves. First they creep along like the others and then suddenly spin round, staves whirling at tremendous speed as if in battle. Mastery of bodily movements, though peaceful in practice, can be useful for combat.

At the centre of the Park is the Temple of Heaven, perhaps the purest monument to Ming architecture left to us. Unlike the Palace architecture, this was designed and built in 1420 for the gods. Here, the Emperor held communion twice yearly with them. At the heart of the complex is the circular Hall of Prayer for Good Harvests. Above its entrance, a huge sign says: 'May the Gods grant a good earth to the farmers.' It is best to approach this from the south. First you come to the Royal Mound or Altar of Heaven on which the Emperor prayed to the gods at the Winter solstice. This circular dais represents earth. Beyond this is the round, blue-roofed Imperial Vault of Heaven. This represents Heaven. Finally there is the Temple of Heaven, a round blue-roofed tower on a circular dais: Heaven on Earth. Enter the blue gate and you will see the Temple half a mile along a raised stone walkway ahead of you, floating above the green gateway. As you approach the gate, the Temple is lost to view. You pass through the second gate and find it hidden behind a third. You pass through this and see it in all its glory, bigger and grander than you had imagined, for while you have only seen two storeys up till now, it is in fact, three storeys high. Three is the key to this temple. Three glazed roofs rest on three sets of pillars, on three steps above three concentric dais, up which mount three stone stairs. Blue pottery tiles, over red wooden pillars, upon a white stone base. Concentric circles within concentric circles, like the earth within the universe. It represents earth reaching up, through the Emperor, to heaven.

The Emperor had a divine mandate to rule China. China was the Middle Kingdom between Earth and Heaven. The Middle Kingdom was created by the legendary P'an Ku, and P'an Ku grew out of an egg which was the beginning of all things. Rather like Alice after eating the magic mushroom, he grew and grew and didn't stop growing for 18,000 years. The shell above him formed the sky and the shell below him formed the earth. After 18,000 years P'an Ku outgrew his strength and collapsed on to the land. His bones formed the mountains, his blood the rivers, his breath the wind, his voice the thunder, and his eyes the sun and moon. The parasites within him formed humanity. The sky stayed where it was. Thus was the world created.

The great wall like an armour-plated centipede on the crest of the hill

The rather undignified rent in the back of the trousers

Shady walkways and a brilliant courtyard

The Son of Heaven was given a heavenly mandate to rule humanity as Emperor. Twice yearly he was obliged to report to the gods how his rule on earth was going and he did this from the Temple of Heaven. A slanting bas-relief set into the first stair depicts clouds – the Emperor was leaving the earth behind him. Phoenixes flutter round the second – he approached Heaven. Dragons entwine round the third – he entered the realm of the gods. Narrowing flagstones on the top dais converge on the temple. Within the temple polished slabs focus on a circular jade stone at the centre. This is the Dragon and Phoenix stone. In its green flecks and swirls lie these mythical animals curled in cloud. From the apex of the roof, a golden carved dragon and phoenix stare down on the stone. Their children, gold like themselves, twist around the blue and green beams of the wall. Massive red pillars, transported from Yunnan Province, support the heavenly roof, floating 104 feet above the ground. The structure is pure. Not a single nail has been used. It is entirely of wood. The calm, cool blue of its hat-like roofs, above the gilded greens and reds of its barrel walls, beneath the crowning golden pinnacle, achieve a rare harmony.

At dusk on the night before the winter solstice the Emperor would get into his sedan chair attended by sixteen bearers and 2,000 courtiers in full regalia. He would be carried from the Forbidden City, down the slightly convex sacred way, sprinkled with golden sand, to the Altar of Heaven. For anyone other than the Imperial Bearers to step upon this way at any time meant instant death, and tonight, all the streets were cleared and absolute silence imposed.

The Emperor rested in a pavilion in the temple precinct until midnight when he rose and dressed in blue to await the dawn. At the proper time, he would proceed to the House of the Ruler of the Universe north of the altar, where he would make the proper prayer. Then, taking the proper number of paces, he went south to stand on the middle of the three terraces of the Altar of Heaven. To the east were placed shrines to the sun, the five planets, and the twenty-eight constellations. To the west were placed shrines to the wind, rain, clouds and moon. Behind him stood the Prompter holding the ancient Book of Rites wherein were contained instructions as to the nature, direction and timing of every detail of the ceremony. On the dais below him was the Tablet of Heaven. On his right and left were the Tablets of the five Emperors attended by ceremonial officers. Everyone was dressed all in blue. Three times the Emperor mounted the topmost dais and intoned the ritual prayer. Three times the ritual music was played. Finally, the chosen bull was slaughtered, and the Emperor carried back along the Imperial Way to the Forbidden City, where he could rest in private luxury until the summer solstice.

Today, a ritual of a different sort is taking place on the same ground, as a kindergarten school performs a traditional dance, laughing and singing the while. Chinese children are happy and well-behaved. I think this is because none of them are ever left out of things. From the moment they are born they are carried around and looked after, but they are never spoiled. No one is spoiled in the People's Republic and everyone is looked after.

As I leave the park to the east I see a crowd of people around billboards. They are reading today's paper. A different page is pinned up against each board.

I go to the railway station. It is time for me to leave Peking, but all my attempts to buy a ticket are ignored or rebuffed. 'Mao, mao. No, no.' I must buy my ticket from China Travel Service and pay three times as much for it as anyone else. I can't even get a meal at a local restaurant. A waiter ceremoniously leads me to the overseas restaurant next door where I must spend a fortune. The authorities cannot understand that some travellers want to live with the people. Some people dislike segregation. It's as if one has been permanently sent to Coventry. They cannot understand that some like to do things for themselves and not have everything done for them by China Travel Service. Perhaps they do understand, but are afraid to help you. What was merely difficult before, is now impossible. Has China changed so much in one year or is this the difference between the provinces and the capital? Although the people are cheerful, there is a tension in the air. This is the political centre of the country. Everything here is political. The people are afraid to step out of line in any way. They may want to help you as individuals, but the system won't allow it, and they are part of the system. Life is not so relaxed here as elsewhere. People still stroll around, laughing and chattering, but there is a slight constraint. It is almost imperceptible as yet, but bodes ill for the future.

I try to visit the Lama Temple. It is closed. Frustration mounts. I cannot see anything in the city, and I cannot leave it. I am trapped.

In common with most other Communist countries, accommodation in Chinese hotels is in double or dormitory rooms. The staff are quite happy to give a single person a room provided he pays the price of a double. Fortunately they do not apply the same principle to dormitories, which perhaps explains why they are so loath to let you stay in them. The staff are equally happy to move someone else into your room without warning. An American businessman called Paul moves into mine. He is an interesting man who teaches transcendental meditation and imports Chinese furniture from Taiwan. He has been looking at factories in China with another importer from Hong Kong. He too has found Peking difficult. In Shanghai, he relates, the workers were all very friendly. They would crowd round and chat to him through his Hong Kong intermediary. The people were genuine and spontaneous. In the Peking factory it was a different story. They were kept waiting for two days. When they finally arrived, the factory was spotless. The workers had spent the previous day cleaning it up in preparation for their visit. They didn't stop to talk but carried on working while he was there. He was shown round by the chief of the works whom Paul felt to be a politician not a businessman. Although he appeared to be friendly, in reality he was not. He told Paul to leave his camera downstairs.

'This was too much', says Paul. 'I was perfectly frank with him. I said – "This is not good business relations. This does not promote harmony. I act on behalf of a consortium. They rely on me for information. If I cannot take photographs, they will not be interested in your furniture and I will not bother to come up." In the end we compromised. I took up the camera and he told me what I could photograph.'

'What couldn't you photograph?'

'There were some things that he obviously didn't want me to see. The outlines of the gold figures on the black lacquerwork were stamped on with a print. Only the detail was done by hand. But I don't hold it against them. On the whole the stuff was better made and cheaper than in Taiwan.'

'Will you buy from them, then?'

'No.'

'Why not?'

'Because things are so difficult in China. You never know where you are. Businesses are run by politicians not businessmen. You may have the money and they may have the product, but unless you make the right noises, they won't sell. All negotiations have to be done between banks. They don't deal with individuals. At the moment there's a six-month wait for delivery. They pretend this is because they are overbooked, but they're not. They just want you to think they are. In Taiwan everyone has their own business. Everyone is a sole proprietor and a sole proprietor will do everything he can to get your trade. It's worth paying the extra money to know where you are.'

Chinese bureaucracy has always been a problem. Government departments interlock and overlap. It takes many days and pieces of paper to get things done. Deng Xiao Ping is attempting to streamline the constitution but some problems will remain, since they are not so much the result of the bureaucracy as the political system. It will always be difficult for communist and capitalist to do business: their minds run along different lines.

I awake next morning with a feeling of groundless optimism. Well, not quite groundless perhaps. Things could not go very much worse than they did yesterday. I succeed in extracting a bowl of noodles from a local restaurant, catching a bus to Lama Temple and sailing only one stop past the one at which I should have alighted.

Yonghegong, or Lama Temple, is one of the biggest Buddhist temples outside Tibet. This is only fitting since it houses one of the biggest wooden Buddhas in the world. In addition to its one huge occupant, it used to hold 1,500 smaller ones, in the form of Buddhist monks. These were all dispersed, however, in the whirlwind of the Cultural Revolution. Now, when China wishes to restore the temple to its former glory and use, Buddhist priests are hard to come by. They've had the spirit knocked out of them and remain buried in rural provinces, working in the fields. A handful of monks have had to be imported from Inner Mongolia. They hold a service early every morning and can be seen wandering around the courtyard in their brown robes. Despite this the temple, like most other temples in China, fails to achieve an air of sanctity. The Chinese are not, and indeed have never been, a religious people. Their lives have been ordered by etiquette and superstition. Perhaps the most basic of Chinese beliefs is Taoism – a form of animism built upon the tradition that the world is made up of two components, 'yin' and 'yang'. Yang is masculine; the sky, life, light, movement, warmth. Yin is feminine; the earth, dark, solidity, stillness, mystery, death. In the ebb and flow of these two forces lies the rhythm of nature. The mystic nature of the Tao, or the 'Way', made it unsuitable as a national religion. A religion which does not believe in teaching or asking questions and which practises inactivity as a way of life is unlikely to make many converts.

The only foreign religion that has made any real impression on China is Buddhism. The teachings of the Buddha came to China from the north-west along the old silk road with traders, around the time of Christ. It has always been strongest in the mountains of the west, but at various times has held influence with the Imperial Court in Peking. Buddhism became, however, intermingled with other more traditional Chinese beliefs, and failed to capture the nation.

The most pervasive and lasting influence on Chinese thought has been the teachings of Confucius born around 550 BC at the same time as two other 'giant' figures of Asian history: Lao Tsu, who founded Taoism, and the Buddha. Confucius translated the order of nature into an order of society based on the twin concepts of service and loyalty: service and loyalty to the family and ultimately to the Emperor. This reinforced the hierarchical caste system and assured reverence to the aged in Chinese society. He made a genuine attempt to find the 'good' life. He believed there is a right decision or action to be made in any situation, which can be reached by applying right principles. His was a calm rational philosophy, rather than a fervid religious doctrine. He set up the ideal of the scholarly civil servant. He devised civil service exams to ensure that the nation would be ruled by talented men. Unfortunately his teachings, dogmatically applied, served to enslave the Chinese mind in a rigid set of formal rules, rather than to free it. With its emphasis on service Confucianism ultimately contributed towards China's susceptibility to Communism.

It is but a short step from the idea of service to an Emperor who embodies the state, to that of service to the state itself. Confucianism also helps to explain the selflessness of Chinese society. Ask a worker if he enjoys his work and he is likely to reply, 'That is not important. My work is useful to the state.' A Westerner visiting China during the Cultural Revolution was shown a formerly prominent nuclear physicist being 're-educated' in the fields. When asked what he thought of his work, he replied, 'My work growing cucumbers for the state is as important as my research in the laboratories ever was.' One may be forgiven for suspecting, however, that the gap between what he thought of his cucumbers and what he said about them may have been considerable. You must always be prepared to receive the state line instead of a personal one when asking sensitive questions in China.

During the Cultural Revolution many of the old beliefs died out. Today, religion is old-fashioned. The young laugh at old people wander round is more of natural curiosity than religious all the answers, and are surprised if a Westerner expresses any belief in God. Hence the atmosphere of the Lama Temple as people wander round, is more of natural curiosity than religious awe.

It is not the buildings at Yonghegong so much as their contents which give cause for wonder. In the central hall is a great seated Buddha. Behind him is a carved model cliff-face peopled by hundreds of figures, with a Buddha in a cave at its centre. Behind this, in the Temple of Ten Thousand Happinesses, is the awesome Standing Buddha, sixty feet high, and carved from a single sandalwood tree dragged all the way from Tibet. The hall is wonderfully dark and dingy. The Buddha towers up from the shadows, covered in layers of dust which have settled in little clouds in the folds of his flaking golden robes. Sombre thankas line the walls while an endless repetition of circles within squares covers the ceiling. He stands staring into the shadows of the upper vaults, oblivious to all beneath.

Rising up from the grey roofs of the town opposite the Lama Temple is another glint of gold. This is the Temple of

Confucius. I make my way to its gates and persuade the slightly hesitant doorman to let me in. A little off the beaten track, this temple makes a pleasing contrast to its more famous neighbour. It has not been restored. While it is commendable that China should seek to repair the demage it caused to its heritage during the Cultural Revolution, it is possible that it will lose something in the very act of restoration. Modern-day artists cannot always catch the delicate tinctures of the ancients. The colours, though perhaps perfectly authentic, seem almost gaudy compared to the muted hues of the originals. In contrast to the brilliant blues and emerald greens of the Lama temple, the vaults of the Confucius temple are midnight blue and scum green. But even here, perhaps we worship a mirage. It is said that the paintings of the Old Masters in Europe, seen in their original state, would seem garish to the modern eye. The faded tints and shades which we so admire today are as much the product of time as of their original makers.

Despite the fact that many of its shrines have been bricked up, the Temple of Confucius retains an old world charm. Amidst the marvellously gnarled trees in the courtyards and standing on the stone backs of giant groaning turtles are tall stele or tablets, bearing in intricate characters the names of the candidates who succeeded in the civil service exams. These date back to the Yuan dynasty (thirteenth century AD). The civil service, and its intricate bureaucracy, ran China for the Emperors for two thousand years. Success in the exams assured one's future career, and any bright student, regardless of birth, could compete. Throughout their careers the top three scholars in the annual exam would be known as Number One, Number Two and Number Three. The man of learning held a position of honour in Confucian thought. The success of this system in securing the services of the most talented to run the Empire contributed to its stability.

In the corridors around the courtyards is a photographic history of old Peking, giving one a glimpse of how the people and monuments looked in times gone by. The photos give us a better picture of life in the past than the monuments and palaces can do. Most of the 'remains' we see today have been rebuilt over the last few years. Admittedly they are restored along the lines of the ancient designs, but how much do temples and palaces really tell us of the past and how people lived anyway? They are misleading. We look at remains in ancient Greece, Rome, Egypt and China, and think we learn about the people who built them. We learn perhaps what they were capable of, but what could an archaeologist in two thousand years' time learn about France from looking at the Eiffel Tower or England from the Post Office tower, or America from the Empire State Building? The millions of slaves and peasants who have disappeared into oblivion, their huts and bones turning to dust, leave not a trace of their existence. We learn something of the top one per cent of any civilisation and no more. If you want to find out about ancient China, look not at the Imperial monuments but the peasants in the fields. Here the people live as they have always done. Here, before your eyes, is ancient China.

After the temple I renew my assault upon the train station. Rebuffed in my efforts to buy a ticket for Xian this morning, I return to the fray – and succeed. My success illustrates the truth of the 'one bite of the cherry' principle. To cajole a ticket out of a Chinese ticket vendor, you are allowed one attempt only, and you must get everything right. One tiny mistake will doom you to failure. From previous encounters I have discovered the time of the train, the number of the counter, the price of the ticket and the fact that you are only able to buy tickets for the morrow after 7 p.m. the previous evening. Armed with a piece of paper detailing all the relevant information in Chinese, I join the end of the appropriate queue. All I lack now is local money. I hopefully flourish my tourist vouchers around in the air, until a Chinaman slightly better dressed than the rest magically appears with a wad of notes, and we quietly make an exchange. Now he has access to the special Friendship Stores and I have access to the ticket vendor.

I think that a nation's queuing habits are indicative of its place in the evolutionary scale of things. They illustrate the extent to which the rational man has overcome the emotional animal. At the top of the ladder are the North Europeans and Japanese. At the bottom are the Indians and Africans. In the middle are the Chinese. The back of a Chinese queue is reminiscent of Japan, and the front, of India. At the very last, the people's patience runs out and they give way to the urge to push and shove. This is annoying and counter-productive. Queue-barging effectively is the theft of a man's time. In the West this is of great importance. In Africa and India it is of less importance. Hence, perhaps, the different attitudes to queuing.

As I near the front, the people behind encourage me to stretch out my long arm: 'Look,' they seem to be saying, 'this is how we do it in our country.' 'No,' I reply, 'that is not how I do it.' They are amazed at my lack of drive, but respect my stance, and kindly refrain from pushing in on me. I slide across my message with the right amount of money, spouting some carefully practised phrases, and am amazed to be rewarded with a ticket.

Back at the hotel, Paul has had a less successful day. He tripped over a stone while paying for a biscuit, sprained his ankle, and sent clouds of money flying through the air.

'I felt such a klux throwing around what must have been a year's wages to them – rather like some king distributing largesse, only this time they gave it all back to me.'

12

The Ancient Capital: Xian

 TRAVELLING by rail in China is always a bit of an adventure. You steam at an easy pace through the countryside with plenty of time to see what's going on, and to get to know your neighbours. It's all very personal. You have your own hard berth with sheets and a blanket awaiting you. The attendant comes round regularly to swab the floor and bring supplies of hot water from the boiler at the end of each carriage for your tea. Why is it that old-fashioned methods of transportation are so much pleasanter than modern ones? Why are sailboats preferable to steamers and steamers to hovercraft, trams to buses, and buses to tube trains, steam trains to diesels, and almost everything to the dreadful internal combustion engine?

We skim across the Shaanxi plateau south towards Xian. This is formed of layers of loess soil from Central Asia, fifteen feet thick in places, dropped by the spring rains. It is a remarkably durable material. Some of the earliest settlements were made by burrowing down into it. Today, sunken houses with distinctive earthen walls can still be seen around Xian. Chairman Mao and his companions, at the end of their 6,000-mile march north to Yan'an, lived in loess caves, and from 1936 to 1947 ran the revolution from them. These are now national monuments.

It is dry and dusty. By dint of labour, the people have turned much of these plains green, but their natural colour is the yellow

160

of the desert. Several of the bridges cross rivers of sand not water. The land, where not yet claimed by man, is covered with a scrub-like growth like the hide of an old camel, worn bare in places. Spring has not yet come to this place. The expanse of the plains is relieved by trees that give the eyes a comfortable vertical anchor in a horizontal sea. Wherever you go in China there are trees. It is one of the country's loveliest features. They line every road and spring out of every courtyard.

There seem to be a lot of trees in China because you see them wherever you look, but they are dotted about, not spread like carpets over the landscape. Any fertile land is devoted to agriculture. In China, while the people believe in Communism, the trees are treated as individuals. In England, while the people believe in individualism, the trees are treated communally.

Xian, or 'Western Peace', lies in the middle of the Guanzhong plain formed by the River Wei south of the Shaanxi plateau and north of the Qinling mountains. It is a strategic position. It is the cradle of Chinese civilisation, and occupies the central role in China's historical development.

Two of the earliest dynasties, the Western Zhou (1100–770 BC) and the Qin (221–206 BC) sprang from the fertile soils of the Wei River plain. Here King Zheng proclaimed himself Qin Shi Huang Di (First Sovereign Emperor of Qin, pronounced Chin) in 221 BC. He it was who first unified China and after whose dynasty the nation gets its name. He conquered the whole 'known world' and bounded it with a wall to the north. He it was who conscripted hundreds of thousands of slaves to build a palace on the banks of the Wei. He was a savage and unbalanced tyrant, whose main concern, having conquered his Empire, was to live for ever. To this end, his courtiers advised him to hide from his subjects and from evil spirits. Sound advice no doubt. Accordingly he ordered not just one palace to be built, but a whole series, joined by covered walkways, so that no one could ever be sure where he was. As a precaution, in case he failed to find the secret of eternal youth, he also started work on a vast mausoleum.

Although his secrecy did enable him to survive three assassination attempts, the mausoleum ultimately was to prove more useful than the palace. His name may yet live for ever, but his body will not. The palace was never completed. The mausoleum fortunately was, just in time to receive the dead Emperor in 210 BC. Deprived of his forceful personality the Empire gave way to popular revolt and three years later, the dynasty which was to last forever was replaced by the Han. The Han established their capital a few miles north of present-day Xian, and called it rather optimistically Chang'an, or Everlasting Peace. Around the time of Christ, the centre of gravity of the Empire moved East, and in AD 25 Luoyang was proclaimed capital. The Han's everlasting peace was disturbed by the Period of Disunion (AD 220–589) which followed. The Sui (AD 581–618) and the Tang (AD 618–907) re-established Chang'an as the capital on the site of the present-day Xian. It enjoyed its heyday under the Tang, when its 2 million population made it the largest city in the world.

A canal linked Chang'an to the Wei which in turn joined the Yellow River. Thus, connected to the rest of China by water, it became the cosmopolitan centre of Asia. The old silk route running from one oasis to the next through the Gobi desert, linked it with yet more distant lands. Thus it was joined to the other great capital of the ancient world: Rome. The interplay of goods and religion along this road was an essential means of communion between East and West. Through the silk road Buddhism was introduced to China. By the same way the guarded secret of silk was introduced to Rome. It became so popular that Emperor Tiberius, around the time of Christ, banned its use altogether. The Chinese traded only for gold and stockpiled this metal in such quantities that it placed a serious strain on Rome's economy. Such was the force that ran along this fragile thread between two worlds. They seemed far removed to their rulers, but they were more closely linked than they knew. Happenings in China had their counterparts in Europe. When China moved against the northern nomads, they pushed west against the Huns, who pressed the Goths, who marched across the Danube and into Rome. Like an air brake, China applied the force and the Roman Empire ground to a halt.

For the most part, however, the silk road provided a peaceful means of interchange between the nations. The Chinese swallowed their traditional distaste for merchants and entertained traders from the farthest lands in Xian. They sweetened he pill, however, by regarding merchants as emissaries. Merchandise was considered to be tribute brought by vassal states. China had a fixed notion of its own superiority, regarding all foreigners as barbarians. Being a barbarian was not so much a matter of race, as of a failure to enjoy the inestimable benefit of Chinese culture. Trade was fairly one-sided. China seemed to have all the materials it needed within its own extensive boundaries. It contented itself therefore with hoarding gold. This self-sufficiency and sense of superiority explain perhaps why they did not pursue further trading links. At one stage under the Ming a vast armada of 28,000 men in sixty-two ships set sail and reached the coast of Africa, returning via India and Java. This was more of an exploratory than a trading mission, however, and though it brought back some interesting novelties for the Emperor, the experiment was not pursued. The Navy was left to rot and China continued its isolationist policy. The silk road was the one communion it allowed itself with the West, and this, depending on the relative strength at any one time of the Empire and the Mongol hordes, was by no means secure. It did, however, account for the prosperity and lively cosmopolitan atmosphere of Xian.

After the glories of the Tang, the city went into decline, and the palaces of the Qin, Han and Tang Emperors turned to dust. The invading Mongols established their capital in the north at Peking in 1271. Xian enjoyed a brief revival under the Ming (1368–1644) but the conquering Manchus who followed preferred the northern site and ruled China as the Qing dynasty from Peking. Here they remained until the end of the Empire in 1911.

The Chinese by tradition have built in wood. That, and China's turbulent history, explains why so few monuments over six hundred years old, other than walls, are left to us. Many of China's finest temples, remains and works of art, having survived for centuries, were destroyed in the Cultural Revolution a mere fifteen years ago. China is now working hard to restore many of the 'ruined' sites, but Xian will never be the same. The ancient capital of China was a natural target for the revolutionaries and one that they did not miss. Despite this, much remains that is worth seeing both within and without the city walls. Much remains still in the ground awaiting discovery.

The shape of the town owes much to the Ming Emperor Hongwu who redesigned it at the end of the fourteenth century. In 1370 he gave Xian to his son Zhu Shuang and had it rebuilt to make it worthy of him. The imposing city walls, twelve metres tall, eighteen metres wide at the base, and with ninety-eight defence towers, were constructed from 1374–78 on Tang foundations. Chang'an had greatly diminished already, how-ever, for the Tang foundations used were not those of the former town limits, but those of the former palace. Much of the blue brick facing has fallen away, but the rammed earth core remains close to its original height. Now trees spring from its crest, and the jumbled tiled roofs of town shops and houses cluster against its sides. Four gates stand at the four points of the compass, their watchtowers and turrets rising up into the granite sky. Bleak and oppressive in their original sombre colours, they frown down on visitors to the city, reminding them of the power of the Emperor.

All Chinese settlements were laid out with great precision by geomancers. It was vital to the wellbeing of the community that the town should be correctly aligned. Main streets criss-crossed in a grid, between which small alleys or *hutong* could run more or less as they wished. At the centre of the old Tang city of Xian stood the Bell Tower. After the city had been redesigned by the Ming, however, it stood too far to the west. In 1582, therefore, it was rebuilt in the heart of town where it stands today. The names of the streets which cross around it tell us something of the importance of the geomantic tradition. On the four points of the compass lie North Street (Beidajie), South Street (Nandajie), West Street (Xidajie), and East Street (Dongdajie). Han buildings had special eave tiles symbolising the different points of the compass. There was Red Bird for south (the most impor-tant point, where the main entrance was always situated), White Tiger for west, Snake curled round Tortoise for north, and Green Dragon for east. Along the white lines in the centre of the roads radiating out from the tower, amidst the buses and bicycles, stand rows of potted plants. What other nation could leave such delicate cuttings unharmed in the centre of its major thoroughfare, I wonder?

I wander through the *hutong* to the Shaanxi Provincial Museum set in the old Temple of Confucius. The halls and galleries round the central garden contain a fine array of early Zhou bronzeware and Tang tri-coloured pottery. At the end of the garden stands the famous forest of stele or engraved tablets. Over a thousand of these remain, covered in intricate carved characters, embodying Confucian and Buddhist classical texts. Some are 2,000 years old. Though Westerners cannot understand what is written, it is interesting to see the development of the various different calligraphic styles. Some of the tablets bear pictures of the great man Confucius himself, and little legends above them. These are the world's first comic strips, perhaps.

I lunch in a dumpling restaurant across the way. Chinese dumplings are round dough-balls filled with meat and steamed in wooden grilled containers like garden sieves. You see them stacked up one on top of the other, ten dumplings in each. I buy a sieve of them, mix up a bowl of soy and green mustard sauce, and set to with a will. It is easy to make a fool of yourself when eating dumplings. The great doughy ball is quite a burden on the chopsticks. Having taken a bite out of one side, the centre of gravity of the dumpling can shift dramatically and send it plummeting down to the bowl of sauce waiting below. This liberally splatters you and perhaps your neighbours with a particularly persistent tincture of soy and mustard. You apologise profusely to your table mates, shamefacedly pick up your dumpling and, in an effort to destroy the evidence, stuff it whole into your mouth. The dumpling, by now saturated with soy and mustard, instantly chokes you, causing still more annoyance and confusion to the poor unfortunates sharing your table.

Relative peace having been restored after one such incident, I return to the task of stuffing dumplings down my throat, resorting to the sauce only in rare moments of confidence, and then at extremely low altitudes. The job is a considerable one, however: ten dumplings take a lot of eating. While experienced hands around me swallow them down with ease, I feel bloated after a mere handful. I gaze despondently at a depressingly large array of dumplings still nestling in a rather obese way in the sieve before me. I soldier manfully through half a dozen and force down a further two before admitting defeat. I am obviously not a ten-dumpling man. In a country where waste is a crime, I climb shamefacedly from my place, and stride quickly from the restaurant feeling like a criminal. Two fat dumplings, an indictment of Western wastefulness, lie redundant on the table behind me.

Weighed down with my burden of dumpling and guilt, I labour off to the Little Goose Pagoda on the outskirts of the town. Just occasionally, the Chinese built pagodas to the gods in stone instead of wood. The oldest of these, built in the seventh century, are the Big Goose and Little Goose Pagodas. No one is sure why they are called the Goose Pagodas. My guidebook helpfully informs me that the Little Goose Pagoda is named after its larger neighbour, the Big Goose Pagoda. While this accounts for its size, it does not explain the Goose. Two equally absurd hypotheses have been put forward in explanation. The first states that Pilgrim Xuanzang built the Big Pagoda to house precious Buddhist texts which he brought back from Asia, and named it the Big Goose Pagoda after a goose-shaped hill on which he lived while he was in India. The second states that it commemorates the strength of some vegetarian Buddhist monks who preferred to starve rather than eat a wild goose which miraculously dropped from heaven beside them.

The Small Goose, like its big brother, was designed to contain Buddhist scriptures, and is all that remains of the Temple of Felicity. The Big Goose is all that remains of the Temple of Grace. Perhaps they were named after twin sisters?

The Small Pagoda is misleading and illusory. It is misleading since, with its 140 foot height and thirteen tiers (six more than the Big Pagoda) it cannot fairly be called Small. In the interests of precision perhaps all reference to Geese should cease and the pagodas be refered to as the Slightly Bigger and the Not Quite So Large Pagodas. The Not Quite So Large Pagoda is illusory because it appears to bulge out in the middle and taper at top and bottom. In ancient pictures it is portrayed as doing just this (like a man who has had one too many dumplings) though in reality, it gets progressively smaller from bottom to top. While the reduction in width between one tier and the next remains constant, the increase in height diminishes; hence the illusion. This is yet another example of Chinese architectural ingenuity. If, while gazing at the Pagoda, you formed the opinion that it was slightly truncated, you would be entirely correct. This is no illusion or architectural trick. The top two storeys toppled off in an earthquake five hundred years ago. That the other thirteen

hild of the Orient

A toothless old man staring at me

The Buddha Fragrance Temple

Trees jut out from the rock at suicidal angles

have remained this long, though restored on several occasions, is a tribute to the skill of the Tang architects who created it 1,300 years ago.

On visiting the Slightly Bigger Pagoda and labouring up the seven flights of stairs within it, I am forced to admit that it is pretty big, though I refuse to see in it any resemblance to a goose. Rising up from the trees of a small mound on the edge of town, it looks very imposing. The view from the top, however, is less uplifting. Where once were fields, now, on three sides are suburbs. Xian's population of two million must live somewhere, but it is a pity somehow, that they live just here.

May is the time of 'little rain' in the Chinese lunar calendar. It heralds the end of the dry season. June is the time of 'great rain'. Today it rains a little, but with great persistence, and drives me back to the hotel where, under the gloom of an overcast sky, I strain my eyes attempting to write. I share a room with an Australian couple called Steve and Sue. Steve is in bed.

'How long have you been here?' is my opening gambit.

'About ten days,' replies Steve.

'That means you either like it a lot, or you can't leave,' I reply jocularly.

To my surprise I am right on both counts.

'Yeah. It's nice, only I've been in bed for a week.'

Witness to this is a great tableful of pills and potions by his bed.

'Look. That's what the Chinese gave me.'

In deference to the sick man who is trying to sleep, I refrain from turning on the light and sit by the window straining my eyes, surrounded by herbal remedies.

'It's no good,' I say, pushing away the book after a bit, 'this is giving me a headache.'

'A headache,' cries Steve joyfully, 'I've got just the thing for that. Here, try some of this. It's powdered Chinese gooseberry, and tastes like Kiwi fruit.'

I hate to point out that the New Zealand national fruit *is* in fact the humble Chinese gooseberry. The Chinese have a knack of pre-dating our proudest achievements by a thousand years or so. I content myself with asking:

'Does it do any good?'

'That's what I asked the doctor,' says Steve, 'but I'm not sure. All he would say is, "It won't do you any harm." And it hasn't either,' he adds as an afterthought.

I mix some up with hot water. It tastes good.

'You haven't any other complaints, I suppose?' asks Steve hopefully.

'Well,' I ponder, not wishing to disappoint him, 'I have got a slightly sore throat.'

'Just the thing. Try one of these,' says Steve, producing a little furry nut in triumph.

I put it in boiling water and it swells to twice its former size, shedding its coat in a waving gelatinous veil like a sea anemone. Steve watches the transformation with immense satisfaction. 'Go ahead, you can try it now.'

'Well, if you're sure it won't do me any harm,' I say dubiously, 'here goes.'

It tastes mildly bitter but not too poisonous. My headache disappears and my throat gets no worse.

'Well, how do you feel?' asks Steve.

'Better,' I reply.

'Well, there you are.'

I resume writing and the headache returns.

Twenty-two miles east of Xian, between the Li mountains and the Wei River, stands a hill, 154 feet high, 3,000 yards in circumference and covered with pomegranate trees. It looks rather peculiar stuck out on its own in the plain, surrounded by fields. It is rather peculiar. It is man-made. It is reputed to be hollow and to contain a subterranean palace with a huge chamber in which is contained a microcosm of the world, with flowing mercury for rivers, jewels for stars, and an eternal flame for the sun. Deep within the palace is another chamber, housing the body of King Zheng, the first sovereign Emperor of Qin, sometimes called the 'Father of China'.

If Zheng was its father, China had a Caesarian birth, coming into the world in a sea of blood. King Zheng ('first sovereign Emperor' was a title which he bestowed upon himself) became leader of the Qin tribe in 246 BC. For the previous centuries the Zhou, driven east to Luoyang, had exercised no more than nominal sovereignty over the area. This was the period of the

Warring States. Culturally, the Zhou still dominated, and collectively the six Warring States, of which it was not one, dismissed the Qin as a barbarian tribe. They were not perhaps so wrong in their judgement, but they seriously underestimated the Qin. The Qin had learned the art of fighting on horseback from the nomad hordes to the north, and with it they were able to defeat the other states, who fought in the traditional way from chariots. Within twenty-five years Zheng had subdued all his neighbours and, for the first time, brought unity to the land. He centralised authority, standardised weights and measures, and drew up a legal code, but remained a barbarian at heart. He established a ruthless totalitarian régime and enforced his commands with a five-fold scale of punishments. For trivial offences (practically anything) there was branding on the forehead, next came the cutting off of the nose, then the feet, then the genitals and finally the head. These punishments were inflicted at his merest whim. All books were burned, save for those on agriculture, medicine and divination. Fortunately much was saved, hidden in the memories of scholars and the walls of houses. Confucian teachers were executed. Knowledge and culture were dangerous and not to be endured. Service to the state was all. There could be no criticism. It is hard not to draw parallels between this period and that of the Cultural Revolution of 1966–76. Both were reigns of terror under totalitarian régimes, during which society was turned on its head and learning desecrated for the sake of the state. The Cultural Revolution, however, was a revolution of the people, while this was tyranny for the benefit of a single man.

King Zheng began work on his mausoleum as soon as he attained the throne aged thirteen. Hundreds of thousands of people were conscripted for the task. A man who could build a 4,000-mile wall and bring the whole known world beneath his sway, and a man with such grandiose designs as King Zheng, would not be content to lie in a mere hole in the ground. Shang monarchs used to entomb live soldiers, slaves and concubines with them at their death, to assist in their after life. When any major building was created, it was considered auspicious to bury a man at the base of each pillar, others outside guarding the floor, and more inside under the floor, and a host of anything up to a hundred, fully armed and with chariots, beneath the approach. Prisoners-of-war were often used for this purpose, though it seems that for particularly important buildings only the sovereign's own men could be relied upon. The Zhou discontinued this barbarous policy, but it was far too grandiose a gesture for a man like Zheng to miss. He was, however, a practical man. He entombed only his concubines and slaves with him, leaving his soldiers for the defence of the realm. For his protection he had a vast life-size army of terracotta soldiers and horses made, each one individually moulded to mirror the features of his own men. Such tomb figurines later became customary amongst the nobility and reached a peak of accomplishment under the Tang. So far, 6,000 men have been unearthed from the ground east of the tomb and no doubt more remain buried in the fields, guarding the other approaches. The terracotta soldiers fulfilled their task. The tomb remains untouched, even today, by the People's Republic. The live soldiers which Zheng so thoughtfully left behind did not do such a good job. The Qin dynasty fell, almost immediately on his death, to a peasant revolt, and was replaced by the Han.

The burial mound rises up from an angular base, forming a circle about a square – heaven above earth. Man has always recognised the purity of the circle, and caught in it a glimpse of the infinite. In it he has found the ideal shape, the music of the spheres and the movement of the stars. Circles hold our society together. Smooth circles, toothed circles, and circles within circles; without them our civilisation would grind to a halt. The circle has indeed a magical quality.

The guardian soldiers are awesome. They stand in lines, 200 metres long. The ones at the rear remain half-buried. Heads, arms and hands stick at strange angles out of the ground, drowning in the dust. The ones at the front wait, wide-eyed and alert. They stare out with a gaze that has not flickered over two millennia. But what are they waiting for? They have stood out the centuries shoulder to shoulder, rank on serried rank, armed and ready for battle. What is the key that will restore them to life? What magical gesture will bring this army leaping and crashing about our ears? Is it the unlocking of the tomb? Were they created 2,300 years ago for this moment? Did Zheng in all his glory see us before him? Time will tell. These soldiers know the meaning of time.

With some justice this has been termed the archaeological find of the century. These soldiers tell us much about life under the Qin. Each one is perfect, with every knot on his shoe and every hair on his head clearly depicted. The crossbowmen are in loose tunics, the swordsmen in thick robes belted at the waist and with a scarf round their necks, the spearmen are guarded with links of armour. The generals, like the Duke of Plaza Toro, evidently found it convenient to lead their troops from behind. Not that King Zheng's troops ever found themselves reversed. It is a formidable force.

China has been inhabited from the very dawn of man's history. Nearly sixty years ago, archaeologists found remains of 400,000-year-old settlements outside Peking. These early precursors of man were named Sinanthropus Pekinensis, or, to the layman, Peking Man. The fertile plains of the river Wei gave shelter to man more recently in Neolithic times, 6,000 years ago. The outlines of their round huts, dug down into the soil with a surrounding protective trench, are clearly visible east of Xian. Inside were found earthenware bowls and a variety of containers – some concealing fish hooks, and others the skeletons of children. The decoration of these bowls reveals an astonishing degree of sophistication. One can see the art develop from realistic portrayal of animals, through geometric, to symbolic forms of representation. Thus a picture of two fish becomes

Chinese art and architecture has maintained close ties with the animal world, both actual and mythological. Dragons writhe around the people's temples, and, wings outstretched, support their roofs. Phoenixes flutter about their eaves and porches, dogs of Fo stand at their entrances and in tiny processions on their lintels and roofs, tortoises support stele on their backs, great-mouthed serpents on the rooftops swallow long lines of tiles, while elephants on the peaks, curl their trunks up into the sky. Tripods stand on elephants' feet, and tables on dragons' claws. In the shops, the pots may have turtle-back lids and the baskets tortoise feet. In the West, art originated in man's urge to portray the wild animals he lived with in crude daubings on the walls of his caves. As it developed it became removed from its bestial beginnings. Chinese art has retained a closer link with its animal origins.

On the way back we visit the hot springs at Huaqing. These rise from the base of the Li mountains nearby and have been the bathing place of emperors for 2,000 years. The mineral waters are supposed to have medicinal properties, though perhaps it was the closest the ancients (imperial or otherwise) ever got to a hot bath. Now it is frequented by lesser mortals and is a favourite resort of present-day Chinese. The springs have taken on a jamboree atmosphere ill suited to the Taoist temples around them.

I go to a local restaurant with some Hong Kong Chinese for a feast. Many provinces in China are renowned for their cooking. Shaanxi is not. Here I discover why. The cooks attempt to disguise the blandness of their food with outrageous spices. One's taste buds are alternately bored then bombarded, and ultimately succumb to a sort of dull numbness.

Back at the hotel, Steve has continued to improve, but Sue has caught his sore throat. Germs in China are spread around liberally by means of the Chinese tradition of communal eating. Tables in Chinese restaurants are large and circular. The diners sit round, each with his own bowl of rice and long chopsticks at the ready. As soon as the food is plonked down in the centre of the table everyone launches in. This promotes great manual dexterity amongst the chopstick wielders, and ensures that a generous helping of food is spread over the table. It also redistributes the individual's germs throughout society in true Communist fashion. Thus everyone in China at this time of year has their share in the nation's ill health – including, in this case, its foreign friends. This does at least ensure a booming trade for China's traditional herbal remedies. We all dose ourselves liberally with these after dinner. Sue, in addition to gaining a sore throat, lost her watch today, and in between medicines regularly asks: 'What time would it be?'

I find her unfulfilled conditional disturbing. Does she mean: what time would it be if I had a watch? Or what time would it be if it's now ten minutes since I asked you last? Or what time would it be if the universe stopped revolving and the earth fell into the sun next Tuesday? I disregard these possibilities and answer in kind: 'I would think it is ten o'clock.'

This happy preoccupation with chronology, together with the wonders of Steve's inflatable coathanger which his mother gave him, makes the hours spin by. The inflatable hanger dries clothes twice as fast as the ordinary variety since its extra thickness separates the material hung upon it. It can also double as a pillow in time of emergency; truly a wonderful device. It is not until I advise Steve that I am aware of the advantages of inflatable hangers that any of us gets any sleep.

Early next morning Steve and Sue pack up their things and, stuffing the deflated hanger (a mere shadow of its former self) into the top of Steve's rucksack, board the 6.30 a.m. train for Peking. Thus aroused betimes, I wander round the old part of town, already alive with activity. The maze-like warrens of old China twist hither and thither with their fluted tiled roofs, lofty mud walls, overhanging timbered eaves, polished stone lintels, secret courts and spreading trees. Life goes on around internal courtyards and behind closed doors. The lanes are so narrow and unfrequented, so far removed from anywhere you could possibly want to go, and so convoluted in shape and design, that it is difficult to pass by inconspicuously. One tries to disguise one's aim, striding purposefully along, intent on keeping some imaginary engagement on the other side of town. The old folk nod sagely as you pass them by, and watch as you are brought up short by a cul-de-sac, to return, head down, the way you have come.

The only clear picture you can get of Chinese village life is from above. Looking down from the Drum Tower in the centre of town I am amazed at the myriad little worlds below me. Protected from all but the eagle's gaze, these families pursue their lives around their tree within their courtyard. The random nature of the sloping roofs and lean-to buildings crammed up against each other, spilling round, over and above their neighbours has a natural harmony. These houses have evolved one from another. Remove one, and the whole edifice will come crashing down around your ears.

The Drum Tower is in an old section of town near the Bell Tower. The great bronze bell was struck every day at dawn, and the drums were beaten for ten minutes before the city gates were closed at night. The Drum Tower looks vaguely like a city gate in that it is a two-storey structure, ninety feet tall, built by the Ming, on a rectangular brick base 170 feet by 120 feet. Today, instead of housing drums, it houses the collection of Xian's leading 'antique' store. None of the articles are very old however, since it is forbidden to export any objects over 150 years old. China has suffered dearly at the hands of enthusiastic Western orientalists and museums who toured the country 'collecting' at the beginning of the century. Whether the oriental treasures thus acquired were saved for posterity or stolen from antiquity remains a matter for dispute between the governments involved. Without doubt much would have been lost in the Cultural Revolution, but equally without doubt much was lost in the Second World War. Regardless of the rights and wrongs of the past, and the advantages to the Westerners of having such things in the West, it would be good to see them now in their original setting.

A narrow lane leads from the Drum Tower to the Great Mosque. I manage to walk straight past this and lose myself in the old part of town. Though much of old Xian has disappeared, some remains. If you seek it out it will frustrate and elude you. If you wander, showing no concern, it will appear and entrance you. In just this lackadaisical fashion I come upon a tiny temple, in the back streets, which formerly belonged to the Town Gods. Today it is a school. I'm sure the Town Gods do not object. Other shrines have suffered a less enviable fate. The Renowned Temple of the Recumbent Dragon, or what remains of it, is now a metal factory.

I find myself on the wrong side of a tall wall beyond which a succession of tiled roofs rise up tantalisingly out of reach. When you get on the wrong side of a wall in China, you are likely to stay there for some time. They normally have but one entrance, which is positioned, likely as not, in the wall diametrically opposite the one you are facing. The Mongols stayed on the wrong side of the Great Wall for centuries. I remain on the wrong side of this lesser relative for some minutes, and, on finally attaining access to the compound, find myself in the Great Mosque.

One may be permitted some slight surprise at finding a mosque in Xian. Mosques in international ports such as

Shanghai are understandable, but here in the heart of China? The explanation lies in the ancient silk road. From the earliest times Arabs made their way across Asia to sell their wares in Xian, capital of the Orient. In its heyday Xian was quite a cosmopolitan community. It was home to merchants, envoys, scholars and priests. Coins from Persia, Arabia, Byzantium and even farthest Rome have been found here. Keen to maintain friendly relations with his foreign friends, the Tang Emperor Xuanzong gave some Muslim merchants permission to build a mosque in AD 742. Restored throughout the centuries, it stands today as an example of the sinification of foreign architecture. Its gateways are predominantly Chinese, its Great Hall Arabic and its fluted roofs and minarets a blend of the two. It is a peaceful compound. A hundred Muslims worship here daily, five hundred on Fridays, and as many as five thousand on the last day of Ramadan. A notice on the wall of the Hall exhorts visitors: 'Please bath before entering.' Another sign reads: 'Toilet head.' Is this some vague insult to the Infidel, I wonder?

Persistent rain and an equally persistent headache drive me back to the hotel. I am prepared to believe that Steve's herbal remedy is not solely responsible for the state of my head, but I begin to doubt the veracity of his words: 'At least it will do you no harm.'

The situation is further compounded by the presence of one Harry in my room.

'Hi, I'm Harry. Pleased to meet you.'

Immediately the phrase Harry the Horse springs to mind. Harry's conduct does nothing to dispel the connotation.

'You a Yank?'

'No, I'm English.'

'On your own?'

'Yes.'

'So am I. I was travelling with a couple of anthropologists, but I had to leave them. They were, you know, unduly large around the cranium area.'

My head is really not at its best. Having exchanged pleasantries, I get into bed and attempt a little writing.

'What are you doing?' asks Harry.

'I'm writing a book.'

There is a slight pause. Sadly, I feel I have just confirmed my own status as being unduly large around the cranium area. His next question is 'You from Oxford or something?'

'Cambridge, actually,' I am forced to admit. Harry smiles triumphantly.

'Got any good photos of Xian?'

'No, I don't have a camera.'

'What? Man, that's unnatural. You're the second Englishman I've come across that doesn't carry a camera. I just can't believe you guys.'

Attempting to explain in suitable words I say, 'I guess we just ain't too crazy on the camera scene.'

Harry seems to accept this as adequate explanation.

'Wow, I've had enough of this country. All the towns are the same. You can't buy anything in them.'

'No, they're not so keen on material things here.'

'I just can't believe it.'

Poor old Harry. There's a lot he can't believe. He's only interested in what he can take away in his camera and mule pack. He goes off to change Hong Kong dollars for Chinese yuan with some Hong Kong Chinese downstairs.

'Man, I'm gonna make some money on this deal.'

Ten minutes later the peace is shattered by his re-entry like a space rocket into the earth's atmosphere.

'Wow,' he bursts in, 'I really screwed them. Look how much I got.' – He has been outsmarted, though I don't care to disenchant him.

Inspired by my literary endeavours, Harry the Horse attempts to write home. He is one of those people who finds it necessary to broadcast at regular intervals what he is doing. He stops every couple of minutes to say:

'Listen to this. How does this sound?'

Ths intervals between each outburst are pregnant with such anticipation that any hopes I have of committing pen to paper are sunk without trace. I give up.

'I'm going to get my train ticket for tomorrow,' I tell him and leave.

On reaching the station, I discover that there is an overnight train in addition to the morning one. A short sojourn on a Chinese sleeper seems a fair alternative to a disturbed night with Harry the Horse, so I buy a ticket for the sleeper. I take the ong way back, meandering through the alleyways of town. 6.30 p.m. is a good time to stroll in China. At that restful moment after the bustle of the day is over, but before the sun is quite gone, the Chinese tend to sit out on the streets eating a bowl of rice, or on the kerb turning the worn pages of a cartoon book at a street-side magazine library, sliding the pieces of a Chinese chess set across a paper board amidst a crowd of onlookers, watering the potted plants, listening to the song of tiny caged birds and chattering to neighbours. In particular it seems a time for the very young and the very old.

I wend my way back to the hotel, and inform Harry that I'm leaving tonight.

'Aw, that's a shame,' he says, 'I was looking forward to a chat.'

Overcome with guilt, I take Harry out to a cheap restaurant nearby where he will be able to eat and congratulate himself on getting a good deal. Having thus done my duty, I say goodbye to the Horse and board my train.

13

Caves and Burrows: Luoyang and Zhengzhou

SCANT HOURS later, or so it seems to me, the attendant wakes me. We are arriving at Luoyang. I attempt to shake the dust from my eyes and the sleep from my head as I stumble out of the station and into the square. It is 5.30 a.m. The sun has not yet climbed above the outline of the surrounding buildings, but already the square is alive. Following the Horse's instructions, I attempt to find a number 10 bus to take me to the Longmen caves. My attempts however cause consternation among the assembled people. They shake their heads morosely: there is no number 10 bus.

To survive in China where so much is a mystery to the Westerner, it is always necessary to have a clear idea of where one is going, one or two accurate pieces of information on how to get there, and, if possible, a note written in Chinese stating your objective. One can get by with two out of the three, but one out of three is a disaster. Thanks to the Horse, I am stranded in a strange town in central China, with a population of one million, and one out of three. I could attempt to find a hotel where someone might speak a little English and start again from there, but that would waste time, and anyway, I don't want to stay here tonight.

I manage, I think, to communicate my destination to the inevitable group of assembled Chinese. One of them brings a motorised trishaw standing nearby and is very intent on getting me aboard. I resist. This is an individual enterprise, especially

178

laid on for the unsuspecting tourist. He is very persistent. 'Get in, get in,' he seems to be saying.

First of all we must fix a price. Not knowing where or how far we are going, this poses a problem. Most people pay at the end of a trip and conduct any bargaining, if such there is to be, then. They feel they bargain from a position of strength. I feel precisely the opposite. In such a situation, I feel in debt and at a disadvantage. I ask him to name his price. He is reluctant to give it, being more intent at this stage to get me into his trishaw than to extract any money – no doubt that will change later on. I remain unmoved, and soon, as I expect, he comes out with a ridiculous price. With nothing other than my assumption of his greed to guide me, I offer him half. He is not happy, but I will not budge. The money changes hands and I climb in.

We scoot through the darkened streets, passing the early morning joggers. Men and women of all ages in China pursue this pastime, which was much encouraged by Mao who described it as good for the circulation. A short while later I am dropped at the bus station and catch a bus to the caves. I have been taken for a ride in more ways than one.

In ancient times, Luoyang used to be one of the great cities of the Empire, surpassed in splendour only by nearby Xian. On a couple of occasions, under the Han in AD 25 and the Wei in AD 494 it actually usurped its illustrious rival to become the capital of the Empire. It declined from the Tang onwards, however, and is now best known for its tractor plant. In the town, all trace of past grandeur is gone, though some remains in the surrounding area.

In the sandstone cliffs of the adjacent River Yi, some five hundred years ago the leading sculptors of the Wei carved a series of Buddhist grottoes. Succeeding dynasties continued the work till over 100,000 Buddhas adorned the walls of 1,352 grottoes. Many of these, sadly, are now defaced. In one, the inevitable Ten Thousand Buddha cave, someone has gone to immense pains to chip off the heads of all the tiny Buddhas lining its sides. This was no wanton act of vandalism, but the calculated destruction of a religion. An instinctive anger wells up against the intolerant Cultural Revolutionaries who committed such an offence. The damage spread to the larger figures too but here, I learn to my chagrin, the fervour of the revolutionaries was pre-empted by that of nineteenth-century European collectors.

Carved into the cliff, and looking from a hillock on the other side of the river for all the world like the home of some giant burrowing creature, the temples retain something of their religious aura. Nothing has been added by man. He has used the cliff exposing only what was already there, locked inside the rock, the giant Vairocana Buddha, fifty-six feet tall, surrounded by his entourage of Bodhisattva, gazes out at the tiny Chinese workers building a bridge across the water towards him.

A Chinese lady who speaks a little English makes friends with me and helps me catch the right bus back to the station. I give her an Evelyn Waugh book which I have finished reading. She is delighted, though, as is always the case with Chinese, I have great difficulty in persuading her to accept the small gift. In a moment of apprehension I explain that the book may seem rather decadent. She doesn't understand the meaning of the word. She makes me write 'decadent' in large letters on a piece of paper for her to look up later. I am rather ashamed of the society the book portrays: the loose living of the English upper crust in the twenties. It will seem like another world to her. I excuse it by saying, 'He exaggerates. English society is not like that any more.'

'What do you mean?'

Grasping for words that she will understand, I say rather feebly, 'It is more equal now.'

'Ah yes,' she says knowingly, 'English society has developed since then.'

Perhaps I ought not to be ashamed of the book. It does, after all, tell her something of life in England. As she pores over it with her dictionary in the future, she will look back and think, 'Did he really come from such a world? Is this what England is like?' All she will have to go on is the one word 'DECADENT' scrawled in large letters across a piece of paper which she uses as a bookmark. It will, no doubt, in a small way, serve to reinforce the belief all Chinese have in their moral superiority over Westerners.

Travelling east to Zhengzhou on the train, we pass through more of the fantastic loess landscape. It seems to be sculptured out of cheese: great slices of ripe Stilton neatly segmented out of he hillside: chasms where an incisive eater has been at work, hollows where a delver has dug. The landscape rises in a confused series of planes and angles defying the dictates of nature. One gorge is filled with fields, another with a sheet of water. The cliffs are riddled with caves, some open, some with doors. Perhaps it is Gouda and not Stilton. 800,000 people live in this surreal loess soil, gradually shaving and remoulding the landscape where it fails quite to suit their purpose. The government encourages this natural form of accommodation. The troglodyte dwellings are horizontal not vertical. From above, one would have no knowledge of their existence but for the strips of verdant green which they coax so surprisingly out of the bright orange soil.

Beside the railway line, buried as if in quicksand, the heads and tails of two ancient stone horses rise out of the ground. Thus they have faced each other over the centuries, drawing neither closer nor further apart, recalling the days when this route was used by a more basic form of transport.

After three hours I arrive in Zhengzhou. This is the oldest of all China's capitals. The earthen rampart which can be seen in the fields outside town, was fashioned 3,500 years ago in the Shang dynasty, 1600–1100 BC. It is sixty feet wide at the base and remains twelve feet high in places. Rammed earth formed the core of most Chinese walls, including the Great Wall built later on in the north. A timber frame was constructed, baskets of earth poured in and, with an army of labourers employed to pound it down, the wall rose up extraordinarily quickly. This was an effective method of construction, as can be deduced from the fact that the wall still stands after 3,500 years. The Shang is the first dynasty of which we have record, and was preceded only by the semi-legendary Zhou. Today Zhengzhou, as capital of Henan province, has a population of one million. It remains a colourful and lively community, its streets lined alternately with green and mauve trees. In England, so they say, you can tell in which direction you are facing by looking for moss on the trunks of trees. In Zhengzhou you can tell by the colour of their leaves. The wide, tree-lined streets do much to relieve the sense of oppression that endless crowded apartment blocks can give in the West.

After lengthy negotiations I manage to secure a cheap room

in an expensive hotel on the outskirts of town – all the others being full. Walking into my room, I see a little desk in the corner with a thermos of hot water and a china cup on it, and a bathroom. Privacy at last. A room with a brew and a chance to write at a proper desk. One is constantly in the public eye in China, and continually the centre of attention. It can become a little wearing at times.

I have a bath, don clean clothes, shave, and offer what I hope is a presentable face to the diners in the hotel restaurant. A Chinaman comes up to my table. He is the guide to a group of Americans staying here and will be sharing my room tonight. In addition he is a teacher of *chi-gong*– the Chinese art of deep breathing. This is supposed to give those who practise it super-human powers of strength and endurance. My friend took it up because he was a weak child. He suffered from asthma and rheumatism and couldn't sleep. Within one month, so he says, he was cured, and now he is a teacher because he wants everyone to enjoy the same benefits. Quite what it can do physically I am not sure, but there is no doubt that many Chinese devoutly believe in it.

My friend practises for an hour before going to bed, and, as if to dispel any scepticism I might have, gives me a demonstration of the power of *chi-gong*. He shows me his hands before adopting his *chi-gong* stance and, taking a massive breath using the whole of his body, he shows me his hands again. The fingers are red and swollen with blood, like over-filled sausages, fit to burst. The effect is dramatic. He encourages me to punch him in the stomach. 'Go on,' he says, 'as hard as you like, I won't feel it,' but I decline, remembering what happened to Houdini.

The next day I set off early with a group of Chinese on a bus to visit Shaolin monastery, built in the shadow of Song Shan to the south-west of Zhengzhou. This is the home of Zen Buddhism where the monk, Boddhidharma, who established this sect, lived in the sixth century AD. Song Shan is the holiest of China's five Taoist mountains. It used to lie at the centre of the Empire. To the north is Hengshan, to the west Huashan, to the east Taishan, and to the south another Hengshan. These mountains represented the limits of the Empire in Qin times and, in consequence, the world. They also represented the five basic elements which Taoists believed made up the world: air water, wood, earth and metal. The world is a mixture of these five. Each can dominate one but is vulnerable to another. Fire melts metal, metal cuts wood, wood grows on earth, earth soaks up water and water quenches fire. These mountains should not be confused with the three holy Buddhist mountains of Emei, Jiuhua and Wutai.

At times, when the Empire was weak, the monks of Shaolin had to rely on their own resources to defend themselves against the world at whose centre they lay. They developed the Chinese martial discipline of Kung Fu and decorated their walls with pictures of its various exercises. With these techniques, the monks defended themselves against brigands from the hills, and Mongols from the north. Their downfall came much later at the beginning of this century, when they supported the losing side in a dispute between local war lords. The conquering soldiers swept into their monastery, as the monks fled to the hills, and destroyed many of the temples. Part remains, however, and the rest is being restored.

As is so often the case on tours, however, the things you haven't been taken to see prove more interesting than the things you have. The three-hour drive through the countryside is the most fascinating part of the trip.

As we sweep through the streets of town at dawn, I notice that the boles of the trees have all been painted white, as if in a British army camp. It reminds me of the advice given by the Sergeant-Major to the raw recruit, 'If it moves, salute it. If it doesn't, paint it white.' If those trees had grown a little faster, they could have been saluted instead of painted. The night soil workers are having a field day. We pass cart after cart, some pulled by hand, others drawn by horse. These people waste nothing. Even the droppings of the horses are caught in little sacks hanging under their tails.

We pass more strange loess settlements on a mixture of levels half under and half over the soil. From each peeps more of the lilac trees which I saw in Zhengzhou. The colours are striking orange, green and lilac.

We stop beside a small group of buildings. By the time the entire contents of our bus has funnelled into one hut ten feet square, I surmise there is more to this than meets the eye. Following them in, I find myself going down stone steps and through a pair of heavy stone doors into the bowels of the earth We end up in a large central chamber, with smaller ones opening off it. This is the tomb of a Han administrator and his family. It comprises a rest room for the bodies, a sitting-room, a dining-room, a meeting-room and even a kitchen. I suppose if one does believe in an after-life, one might as well go the whole hog. But where is the bathroom, I wonder?

We journey on and approach the mountains. The land is very arid here. As we reach the foothills the plains turn to dust. A harsh wind gusts down the valley kicking up plumes of sand On a bluff overlooking a village is a tumbledown wall and a large stone tablet. Tall and lonely, propped up by a tree trunk it stares out over the plains like a crippled sentinel. It was placed here 2,400 years ago, so the legend on its side relates This is one of the earliest centres of learning in the country founded in Shang times. The wall surrounds some ramshackle farm buildings, in the midst of which stand two gnarled cypress trees. These, planted over 3,000 years ago, are amongst the oldest trees in the world. Dry, twisted and split, you would take them for desiccated husks devoid of life, were it not for the sprigs of green sprouting from their upper branches. This year, like every other, they are responding to the call of spring. How much longer, I wonder, will they be able to draw forth life from the soil?

We continue to Shaolin monastery. This would be quite interesting were it not a Chinese tourist resort. Noisy crowds fill the courts and temples, transforming the peaceful retreat into a place of noise and confusion. Surprisingly the Chinese people do not seem unduly interested in their antiquities. Perhaps they are so much surrounded by the past in their ordinary lives, that particular examples of it fail to catch their attention. They prefer the colourful and slightly garish restorations to the faded originals. The Chinese are giving a facelift to many of their most famous monuments, and have plans to turn old Xian into a sort of oriental Disneyland. These temples and monuments, once restored, suffer an essential change, not just in their appearance but in their nature. They become public property. Now thousands of Chinese shout and climb all over them. How can these people with their Confucian traditions be so out of touch with the spirit of a place? I used to think the Chinese a spiritual people. Now I am not so sure. The neo-Confucian revival placed great emphasis on humanity, and the Chinese today are much more interested in themselves than their surroundings – hence their fetish for photographs. You have to queue up to see anything behind a crowd of cameramen. When you actually get a chance to see a thing for yourself, the people look at you in surprise. Where is your camera? When they realise that you are merely looking and not photographing anyone, someone soon steps in front of you, and business is resumed. What is more important: seeing something or photographing it? There is no doubt in my mind and, equally, none in a Chinaman's.

On the way back I manage to get a seat at the front of a bus. This has the obvious advantage of enabling one to look out of the windscreen at the surrounding countryside, but, in China, the concurrent disadvantage of being next to the driver's horn. Chinese drivers rely more on sound than sight when piloting their vehicles. Lights and indicators, if provided at all, are never used. Perhaps this is because most of the traffic one meets on the road consists of bicycles and carts. Drivers constantly swing back and forth across the road, avoiding these more pedalling forms of locomotion, never bothering to think that there may be other traffic behind, or even in front, unless a blaring horn brings it to their attention. It takes a degree of sophistication beyond which the Chinese have presently reached, to rely on sights rather than sounds to indicate one's intention on the road. Thus the bus horn is continually in use and, being positioned inside the vehicle, is more annoying to the passengers than to those outside the bus. The cyclists continue in a straight line, quite unperturbed. They have pride of place in the Chinese transportation system. The passengers, on the other hand, are driven to distraction – at least I am. I resolve never to go on a guided tour again – local or otherwise.

Zhengzhou is a great junction in the Chinese rail system. From here one can catch trains direct to the furthest flung parts of the realm – and people from the furthest flung parts of the realm accordingly find themselves standing in long lines in Zheng-zhou station hall. The queues reach tremendous dimensions, quite out of proportion to the relatively humble size of the city, but commensurate, one feels, with its possible catchment of a billion people. I find myself at the rear end of one of these prodigious queues snaking round the interior of the station hall. Rather like a Chinese dragon swallowing its tail, the queue coils round the building and seems to catch up with itself again, so one is never very sure whether one is at the front, in the middle or at the end. It is my experience in such situations that foreigners invariably find themselves at the end of the line. My pessimism proves to be not entirely without foundation. As the queue begins to move, the people directly behind me are disgorged easily out of the hall door, while I find myself describing a neat circuit around the perimeter, passing exactly the same spot I'd been standing on five minutes previously, before issuing in turn out on to the platform. Chinese train-queues have this at least to recommend them. While you may spend lengthy periods of time in a state of complete immobility, when you begin to move, you do so with extreme rapidity. The train has a limitless capacity to consume the steady stream of passengers which tumble through its doors filtering thence from one carriage to another down its endless line. Spaces miraculously appear on the seats, and soon the whole vast congregation is housed. One feels that the train can accommodate exactly as many people as care to come. No burden is too great for the engine, and with a tremendous puffing and blowing of pistons and rods the clanking giant heaves itself into motion. Unfortunately, a good deal of the soot and smoke has transferred itself from the engine to the windows of the train. While the floors of the carriages are kept scrupulously clean by the regular mopping of attendants, the same cannot be said of the fenestration. This sad fact serves considerably to obscure my perception of what is going on in the world outside, limiting me to observation of my more immediate surroundings, and an introspective look at my own journey home.

The Chinese seem quite happy to combine different forms of transport at the same time. Through the gloom of the window I am surprised to see a string of buses sweep by – on the back of a train. Further on, I see a man walking along a disused railway line, across a river, carrying a bicycle. It is a curious phenomenon, but one which I have noticed on occasions when travelling in the past, that the longer one spends in transit whether by train, ship, coach or plane, the greater is one's independence sapped, and the less inclined one is to get off at the end of the journey. The thought of having to do something for oneself, at the end of the journey home instead of sitting back and letting things happen, is almost too much for me.

The Chinese have a saying: 'A journey of a thousand miles begins with a single step', but who is to say where a journey really begins or ends? Travel shows that there is nothing inevitable about one's passage through life. There are always alternatives to the track one is on. For many people these run parallel, forever inaccessible, but the traveller sometimes manages to bend his way along them. Further tracks open out before him and an endless variety of routes present themselves. They would take lifetimes to explore and more. His train might shunt into a sleepy little siding and lose forever the main stream, or be misdirected down the wrong track, all unknowing till it came to the end of the line. The most important thing is to find the correct line and follow it.

Who knows whether the Chinese or Western route is the better? Now at last there is a line between East and West; it is up to us to travel along it and see for ourselves.

Index

188

DATE DUE

Demco, Inc. 38-293